First published in 2000 by MBI Publishing Company, 729 Prospect Avenue, PO Box 1, Osceola, WI
54020-0001 USA

MBI Publishing Company books are also available at discounts in bulk quantity for industrial or sales-promotional use. For details write to Special Sales Manager at Motorbooks International Wholesalers & Distributors, 729 Prospect Avenue, PO Box 1, Osceola, WI 54020-0001 USA.

Library of Congress Cataloging-in-Publication Data

Rafferty, Tod.
    Ducati / Tod Rafferty.
      p. cm.
    Includes index.
    ISBN 0-7603-0663-X (hb: alk. paper)
    1. Ducati motorcycle—History. I. Title.
TL448.D8 R34 2000
629.227'5'0945—dc21   99-089138

On the front cover: More than a few 916 owners were first in line to trade up to the 996 in 1999. Among them was Ross Putnam, who was kind and silly enough to offer his new machine for book photography. Joe Carrillo was the rider/model for the session. *Bill McMillan*

On the frontispiece: This logo is on the fuel tank of Clinton Kendall's 1974 "Imola GT."

On the title page: Carl Fogarty puts the Ducati 916 Superbike racer through the paces at Laguna Seca. *Bill McMillan*

On the back cover: Top: The 750 GT first appeared in 1971. Bruce Finlayson's restored 1974 has been lightly modified with Sport pistons and 32mm carburetors. *Bruce Finlayson* **Bottom:** Mike Hailwood at age 19 on the 125 Ducati desmo twin.

Endpaper: Numbers 270, 271, and 269 on the line for a 1956 race.

Edited by Lee Klancher
Layout by Jim Snyder
Designed by Tom Heffron

Printed in Hong Kong

CONTENTS

DEDICATION

This book is dedicated to Fabio Taglioni

and in memory of Gianni Degli Antoni, Renzo Pasolini, Jarno Saarinen, Mike Hailwood, Jimmy Adamo, and Michael Paquay

"The best of Italian design seeks a visually successful way to integrate and arrange the elements of a useful object. It is based on reality, and not on denying or concealing it. The goal is to create a thing that is beautiful in its use and not just in the abstract."

—*Kevin Cameron*, Cycle World

FOREWORD

I've always thought that if creation of the world's motorcycles, through some bizarre shift in the time/space continuum, had been farmed out to history's great artists, Ducatis would have been designed by Michelangelo. I think it's safe to say that in the small, secular sport of motorcycling they are the closest thing we have to the ceiling of the Sistine Chapel.

Leonardo da Vinci might have done the first technical drawings and conceptualized their spare mechanical logic, but we'd have to leave it to Michelangelo to breathe vitality and color into their final form, to illustrate the passing of the divine spark that separates real art from ordinary work.

Ducatis are something special, a little bigger than life. From the beginning, they have always gone a step beyond mere utility or engineering cleverness into the realm of passion. There have been some downright ugly Ducatis, a few odd ones, and more than a couple withered—or mercifully pruned—branches of the evolutionary tree, but the best ones stand on the pinnacle of what can be done with metal, fiberglass, high-spirited ideas, and red paint. Or silver and duck-egg green paint, in some cases. The good ones are legendary.

As Phil Schilling has pointed out, the early Ducati legend really rests on three pillars: Paul Smart's unexpected 1972 victory in the Imola 200 on what became the 750 SS; Cook Neilson's 1977 Superbike win at Daytona; and Mike Hailwood's return-from-retirement romp at the Isle of Man Formula One race in 1978. David and Goliath battles all, in which the efforts of a few inspired people turned back the forces of the great corporate steamrollers. And the vision behind these victories came from a single modest man, the equally legendary Dr. Fabio Taglioni.

Perhaps we are just hungry for recognizable individuals who do great things, but it's a fact that Ducatis have been the weapon of choice for successful racers who tilt at windmills, right up to the present, with Carl Fogarty—who rides like a force of nature—and his beautiful red 996. Some might debate whether modern Ducatis still deserve their underdog status after a decade of stunning success, but no one will deny that they have achieved their goals through persistence of vision and an unflinching loyalty to engineering concepts of balance and lightness.

In any case, Ducatis are—and have always been—more than just tools for winning races or vehicles for personal transportation; they seem to have been put on earth to make life interesting.

Which is why I've owned seven of them myself. And why you can never have too many good Ducati books to read, or too many good Ducati photographs to ponder and enjoy. Like the bikes themselves, the words and pictures here go straight to that magical interaction between the heart and the mind—the stuff that makes life worth living.

—*Peter Egan*

ACKNOWLEDGMENTS

The author would like to thank the following people for their help in creating this book: Henny Ray Abrams, Rob Allen, Joe Anastasio, Dan Argano, Bruce Armstrong, Ludovica Benedetti, Massimo Bordi, Ben Bostrom, Fat Burns, Kevin Cameron, Don Canet, Bobby Carradine, Joe Carrillo, Paul Carruthers, Nick Cedar, Doug Chandler, Pierfrancesco Chili, Troy Corser, Claudio Domenicali, Colin Edwards, Peter Egan, Bruce Fairey, Eraldo Ferracci, Bruce Finlayson, Carl Fogarty, George Fogarty, Anthony Gobert, David Gross, Gary Grove, Ian Gunn, Wayne Harrison, Henry Hogben, John Huetter, Gordon Jennings, Larry Kahn, Clinton Kendall, John Laughney, Jim Leonard, Rino Leoni, Marco Liconti, Diane Mayfield, Chris McCleary, Bill McMillan, Tom Meadows, Federico Minoli, Marco Montemaggi, Michele Morisetti, Cook Neilson, Dennis Pegelow, Larry Pegram, Doug Polen, Ross Putnam, Jim Quaintance, Bronwyn Rafferty, Dan Reeser, Tom Riles, Kenny Roberts, George Rockett, Clement Salvadori, Kristin Schelter, Phil Schilling, Gary Schmidt, David Scott, Cristiano Silei, Jack Silverman, John Stein, Davide Tardozzi, Pierre Terblanche, Malcolm Tunstall, Leeann Tweeden, Terry Vance, Doug Van Tassel, Alan Volbrecht, Guy Webster, and Jonathan White.

Thanks also to Rod Davis, Laguna Seca Raceway; John Cardinale, Sears Point Raceway; and Les Phillips, Buttonwillow Raceway.

INTRODUCTION

Ducatis are seductive motorcycles. Italy has produced or designed most of the sexy cars and motorcycles built in the past 50 years, but only two Italian companies, Ferrari and Ducati, have achieved much commercial continuity worldwide. That's because Italian design/engineering/production decisions are rarely based on market surveys, and because they can't help going racing. From the Roman chariots on up through the centuries to the Testarossa roadsters, this lust for speed has animated Italian design. And while this approach hasn't always ensured market viability, not racing has only proven to damage the merchandising efforts. Thus has Ducati, for more than four decades, been mostly about racing.

When engineer Fabio Taglioni came to Ducati in the mid-1950s, the dominant Italian builders were Aermacchi, Benelli, Gilera, Garelli, Laverda, Mondial, Morini, Moto Guzzi, and MV Agusta. All owned their share of racing success, and challengers could expect demanding tests. Taglioni's first overhead-cam singles made their marks quickly, and were soon followed by his desmodromic valve system, which became once and forever the benchmark feature of Ducati engines. The engineer's design signature distinguished the Bolognese bikes for his nearly 30 years as technical director, and has been carried through in the current generation of V-twins.

The history of corporate management at Ducati has been less consistent. In the mid-1980s, when it appeared Ducati would succumb to government-mandated reorganization, Cagiva stepped in as savior and provided another 10 years of economic survival and racing development. Then, in the mid-1990s, when Cagiva found itself overdrawn and forced to put Ducati on the market, the U.S. Texas Pacific Group became the new owners. Throughout these four decades and peaks and valleys of economic vitality, one principle held constant in Bologna: Build fast and reliable racing motorcycles, then modify them for road use, rather than vice versa. This seems to be working.

That's our story up to now, told more fully in the following pages, and even better by the many superlative photographs of Ducatis at speed and in repose. In some you may see the unity of line, shape, balance, and stance that defines Italian design sensibility at its best. In others you can glimpse the extraordinary dynamic of rider and machine dancing at the edge of possibility and chance. Among the herds of mechanized horses now on hand for the everlasting rodeo, the Ducati remains one of the few genuine thoroughbreds.

—*Tod Rafferty*

CHAPTER 1

Capacitors to Puppies

1926-1948

The Ducati story has more twists and turns than a bowl of rotini pasta. Since before the Roman Empire, Italy has been fractured by foreign invaders, political factions, assorted marauders, and zealots. Which makes all the more remarkable the numbers of fine Italian cars and motorcycles built in the past 70 years. Plus, the distinctions between art, science, and commerce have always been loosely defined in Italian culture. In school we learned of the great Renaissance in Italy, and the immortal names of da Vinci, Michelangelo, Botticelli, Ferrari, and Taglioni.

Ducati began in 1926, between the first and second installments of the World Wars. Italy succumbed to the specious appeals of fascism after the first round in 1919, effectively dooming itself for the second one. But the Mussolini government did set the framework, albeit artificial, for industrial stability in northern Italy, and the brothers Cavalieri Ducati were poised to start a company. Adriano, the oldest at 23, and brothers Bruno and Marcello set up shop as the Ducati Patented Wireless Company to make vacuum tubes, condensors, and related components. The motorcycles were yet 20 years in the future.

Together the Ducati brothers combined their talents for technical innovation, management skill, and design sensibility, and the company grew steadily. By 1935, with markets throughout Europe, they moved to larger facilities outside Bologna, where the firm produced cameras,

The Ducati Museum, opened in the summer of 1998, offers the Ducatisti an engaging and informative stroll through history.

The brothers Cavalieri Ducati—Bruno, Marcello, and Adriano—created the Societa Radio Brevetti Ducati in the summer of 1926. Adriano, then 23, had been a physics student and admirer of fellow Bolognan Guglielmo Marconi. Marcello was the designer of the group, and Bruno the administrator.

radios, cash registers, and electric razors. By 1939 the Ducati factory employed more than 7,000 workers.

Mussolini initially declared Italy neutral in World War II, but in 1940 allied with Germany against France and Britain. When Mussolini was ousted in 1943, Italy signed an armistice with the Allies, but the northern third of the country remained under Nazi control. Since the Ducati factory was then manufacturing components for military hardware, it became a target for Allied bombers, and was partially destroyed in 1944. Italy was reunited by liberation in 1945, and a republic replaced the monarchy the following year. In the elections of 1948, with considerable persuasion from Britain and the United States, the Italians elected a strongly anti-communist government.

Their economy had been wrecked by the war. Italy's holdings in Yugoslavia and Ethiopia were gone, and added claims from Greece and the Soviets produced a bill for $3.5 million in reparations. The government-controlled Institute for Reconstruction of Industry took over many companies considered essential for the restoration of the economy, among them Ducati and SIATA of Turin. During the German occupation, the Italian Society for the Application of Auto/Aviation Technology had developed a 48-cc four-stroke engine as a bicycle attachment. Designed by Turin lawyer/engineer/writer Aldo Farinelli, the little aluminum engine weighed 17 pounds and delivered 150 miles per gallon of precious, and expensive, postwar fuel.

Farinelli's tidy little engine emitted a staccato yap that would establish its name, the *Cucciolo*, or Puppy. The clip-on motor was an immediate success and soon strained the production capability of SIATA, whose primary business evolved from building high-performance Fiats to producing complete automobiles after the war. Under the government's plan for industrial reconstruction, the Ducati plant was rebuilt in 1946 and Cucciolo production shifted from Turin to Bologna. As the Cucciolo developed into a full-fledged moped, Farinelli was granted a royalty on each engine. The Ducati brothers received only nominal compensation in the deal, and shortly after emigrated to Argentina. Only by historical accident would the family name be affixed to motorcycles.

The marriage of Farinelli's little pup and Ducati's engineering and manufacturing capability was fortuitous. With its 9-mm Weber carburetor and 12-mm valves controlled by pullrods, the engine churned out 1.25 horsepower. The Cucciolo offered thousands of Italians their first motorized transport, with a top speed of almost 30 miles per hour. Times were getting better.

Within a year Ducati held a 50 percent share of the moped market and was expanding its sales network throughout the rest of Europe. Most of its competitors, foremost among them Garelli, built two-stroke engines that required gas/oil pre-mix. The greater torque and minimal maintenance requirements of the Cucciolo made it a popular choice in the hills of Italy. In three years of production, the Bologna factory turned out

nearly 100,000 barking puppies, and in another two years had doubled that figure.

Now the time had arrived for the young company to offer a complete motorcycle. Rather than contract an established chassis builder, the government's industrial directors (a lingering fascist tradition) appointed Aero Caproni, an aircraft manufacturer, to build motorcycle frames. The Cucciolo was then in its second generation (T2), and the 65-cc TS would appear with nearly twice the horsepower and an additional 10 miles an hour in hand. The 100-pound Ducati/Caproni had a pressed-steel frame, rode on 22-inch wheels, and breathed through a 15-mm Weber carburetor. And it was quite stylish.

But after less than a year as partners, Caproni decided to build its own motorcycle, the Capriolo, and became Ducati's competitor. With additonal pressure in the form of motor scooters from Piaggio (Vespa) and Innocenti (Lambretta), the Bologna company began losing

The Cucciolo was cute as a puppy and had its own theme song, which became a popular tune and had Italians whistling in the streets. Motorcycle advertising of the late 1940s was based on the fundamental appeals and benefits of fun and economy combined.

The Cucciolo engine began as a clip-on that would run efficiently on the scant and low-octane fuel available after the war. Its first upgrade came in 1948, with a low-compression utility version and a high-compression Sport model. Note the pullrod valve mechanism.

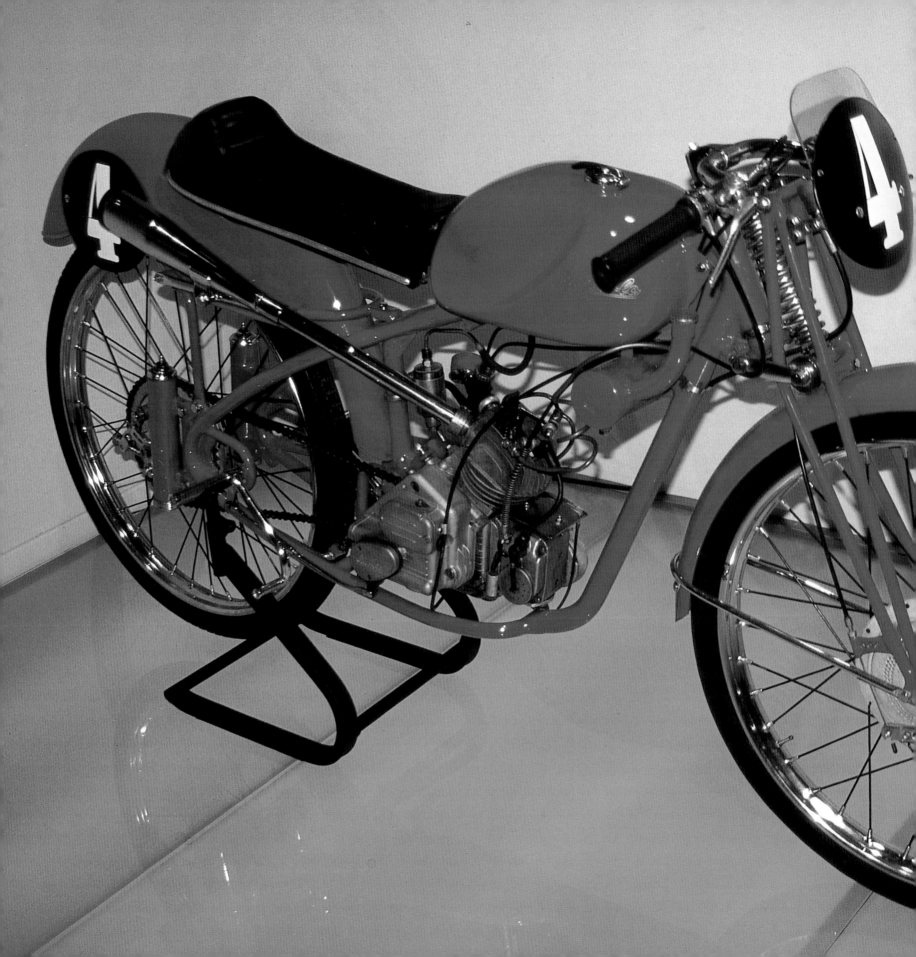

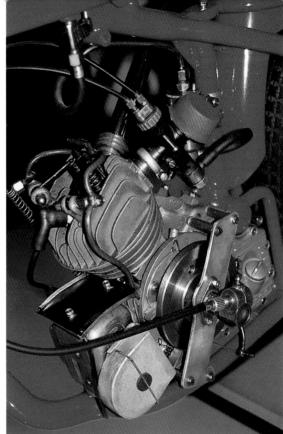

its dominant position in the market. Ducati suddenly found itself a necessary mother of invention and quickly moved to consolidate the talent available in-house to produce all the components for a small motorcycle under its own direction and control.

The Cucciolo remained in production to satisfy the economy requirements of a country still struggling under reconstruction. The proliferation of motorized two-wheelers moved the government to restrict mopeds to a top speed of 22 miles per hour. But Italians had a long-standing predilection for higher velocities.

Giovanni Fiorio had redesigned the Cucciolo as a 65-cc pushrod engine, which would power the model called the Ducati 60. The new machine was offered in standard form and the upscale Turismo version, with footboards, leg shields, and a partially enclosed engine. Both models featured a three-speed transmission and friction damper rear suspension. The 60 represented the transition from moped to small motorcycle, with its kick-starter, leading-axle telescopic fork, and 18-inch wheels. The new model was good for nearly 40 miles per hour.

Then, apparently convinced in advance of their impending success in the newly competitive market, Ducati's directors applied a delightful bit of Italian logic. They decided to go racing.

The first thing to do with a new model, as all Italians knew, was to enter some races to prove it out. The Cucciolo racer established its capabilities early on in the lightweight championship events, and the Ducati marque gained attention quickly. Larger engines with more gears were forthcoming.

53

1955 1957 1958 1959 1960 1961

MIANI RECCHIA: I primi eroici piloti Ducati / the first Ducati heroes

201

4

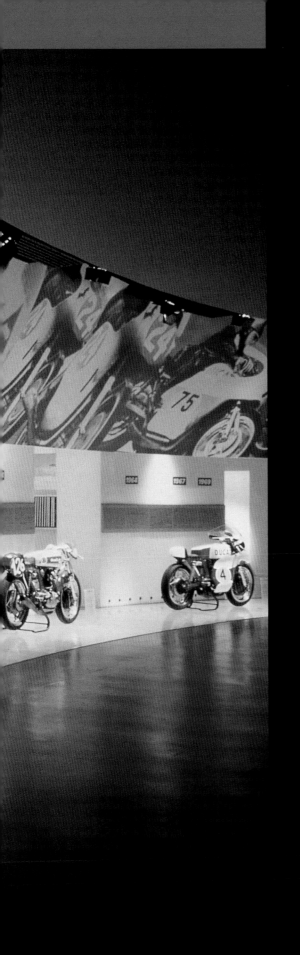

CHAPTER 2

Mopeds, Racers, and Roadsters

1950-1959

Italians love racing of any kind, and wasted little time getting back to motorcycle competition after the war. Even though most of the machines were the spidery bicimotores, powered by 50-cc Cucciolo and Alpino engines, the time had come to have some fun in the streets. The races through Milan and Bologna caught the public fancy, and with the improving economy came time and money for recreation, and racing heroes.

The dashing Ugo Tamarozzi was king of the Cucciolisti, a veteran tuner and rider whose race-face included a smoking cigar. In 1951, at the age of 46, Tamarozzi set 12 world records in the 50-cc class, including an average of 41 miles per hour for 100 miles. Italy hosted the International Six Days' Trial in 1951, and Tamarozzi rode his Cucciolo to a bronze medal.

Ducati chief engineer Giovanni Fiorio built an even stronger puppy, and Tamarozzi raised the 10-kilometer record to 48 miles per hour. But the ensuing performance in the 800-mile race from Bezol to Taranto was disappointing, when none of the six privately entered Cuccioli made it past the halfway mark. Ducati's speed and distance records stood nonetheless for five years, and

The Ducati Museum rotunda contrasts the colorful machines with dramatic enlargements of black-and-white historical racing photos.

Le caratteristiche e le prestazioni del « CRUISER » Ducati erano fino a ieri, un privilegio di alcune rare automobili di gran lusso; oggi tali caratteristiche e prestazioni sono raccolte in un veicolo che interesserà la innumerevole schiera degli appassionati delle due ruote.

Gomme
PIRELLI

The Cruiser was technically interesting, but the complex design and elaborate drive system made it prohibitively expensive. The 175-cc four-stroke engine carried an electric starter and hydraulic drive system, which combined to make it a fairly heavy scooter. Top speed was 50 miles per hour.

the Cucciolo carried on into the mid-1950s as an economical and reliable transporter. The final 55E models had 65-cc engines, real shock absorbers, and a top speed of 45 miles per hour.

Benelli, Gilera, and MV Agusta had established the connection between racing victories and motorcycle sales. But despite numerous records of its own, Ducati had yet to consistently prove its mettle in the demanding arena of international competition. Giuseppe Montano took the position as Ducati's director in 1951, and sport riders were pleased to hear that the new man was also an enthusiast, and supported the creation of a racing program. But two separate and distinct projects were in process at the time, one a 98-cc single that made 6 horsepower, and the other a unique 175-cc four-stroke single in a motor scooter called the "Cruiser." The Cruiser was built to gain some of the blooming scooter trade ushered in by the Vespa and Lambretta. The transverse, horizontal engine featured an automatic transmission with a hydraulic torque converter to engage direct drive, and an electric starter. Thus the Cruiser was rather heavy, and the innovative transmission worked poorly in traffic or on mountain roads. The scooter lasted only two years, ensuring its contemporary status as a collector's item.

The 98-cc engine appeared in the 98 Sport at the Milan Show in 1953. While the Cucciolo remained in production, the new pushrod engine signaled Ducati's intent to build more sporting machines. The standard 98 was still a utilitarian device, with its pressed-steel frame, a 165-pound motorbike good for about 50 miles per hour. But the S and SS sport models weighed less, and had an oil cooler and more compression and horsepower. The sporties were closing in on 60 miles per hour, and both Alberto Farne and Giovanni Malaguti finished the 1954 Welsh Six Days' with silver medals on the 98 Sports.

In 1953 the national directorship divided Ducati into separate entities. Ducati Meccanica occupied the traditional Borgo Panigale factory, and Ducati Elettronica was situated a few blocks away and under separate management.

The 1950s saw user-friendly motor scooters expand to dominate the utility segment of the market. Dr. Montano had obviously committed Ducati to a sporting role among motorcycle enthusiasts, and by 1953 he noted the need for an engine more sophisticated than the 98. Gilera and Moto Guzzi were the dominant Italian builders in world-class racing at the time, and Mondial was on the top shelf in 125-cc competition. The double overhead-cam engines of Alfonso Druisani often outpaced 250-cc machines.

And it was at Mondial that Montano found an engineer eager for new challenge, a graduate of Bologna University named Fabio Taglioni. The engineer was pleased at the chance to design a new engine.

Italy had no shortage of capable designers or outstanding racing machines in the 1950s. International roadracing pitted Gilera, MV Agusta, and Moto Guzzi against the powerful German machines from NSU, DKW, and BMW; the British Velocette and Norton firms also produced strong racing motorcycles. Montano and Taglioni agreed on the prudence of staying with the smaller displacement categories, where the underdog might still have a fighting chance.

Their targets were the 100- and 125-cc classes, then the domain of the Gilera double overhead-cam four-stroke and the Morini two-stroke. Taglioni was effectively the new kid on the block, although he was 33 years old, and his drawing board was unencumbered by previous engine designs. He was assigned the task of designing and overseeing the production of small-bore engines with a high-performance profile and the broad flexibility required for reliable application on the road.

Desmodromic Duetto

Ingenere Taglioni had considerable experience with overhead-cam, single-cylinder racing engines from his years at Mondial. The four brothers Boselli had built their first double overhead-cam, 125-cc singles just after the war, and Mondial captured the world title three years running. But the early 125s were rather large and heavy, and Taglioni knew they could be improved. The more serious challenge would come from MV Agusta, whose first four-strokes had appeared in 1950. MV had

Taglioni's debut design was the Gran Sport 100, known as the Marianna. Within two months of its release, Gianni Degli Antoni took the overhead-cam racer to the class victory in the demanding nine-day Motogiro d'Italia. The 100-cc engine made 9 horsepower at 9,000 rpm.

Engineer Taglioni (center) confers with the test riders at Imola in 1955. That success had come so quickly with the new engine surprised him, and he became an instant hero in Bologna. The bevel-drive overhead-cam racers were sophisticated engines compared to most of the competition.

recently become a strong contender by winning the 125 title in 1952. The mighty NSU racers from Germany included the elegant double overhead-cam Rennmax, which had taken rider Werner Haas to the 125 and 250 world titles in 1953.

But history often rewards the underdog. NSU retired its factory effort in 1954 and the 125 contest came down to Mondial and MV. For 11 years, from 1950 through the 1960 season, Carlos Ubbiali and the MV never finished below third in the series and took the championship six times. But in 1958, Alberto Gandossi and Luigi Taveri, the latter a former MV rider, came second and third on Ducatis in the 125-cc division. MV's emphasis had recently shifted to the more prestigious 250-, 350-, and 500-cc classes.

Taglioni had first drawn up a fairly straightforward 100-cc single, the cylinder canted forward at 10 degrees, with a single gear-driven overhead cam and geared primary drive. The 9-horsepower engine had a 20-mm Dell'Orto carburetor, four-speed close-ratio transmission, and 17-inch wheels. The only external clue to its intention were the words cast into the cam cover: *Ducati 100-cc Gran Sport*. The later 125-cc racing

3° GIRO MOTOCICLISTICO D'ITALIA 1955 - In
BATTILANI - VIGHI - ING.TAGLIONI -
VILLA e LELLI

Giuliano Maoggi shows intense determination as he rolls to the line for the 1956 Motogiro d'Italia. Maoggi won overall honors on the 125 Gran Sport, outpacing the 175-cc entrants. Alberto Gandossi won the 100-cc class for Ducati, and the Bolognese bragging rights were secured.

Leopoldo Tartarini (left) and Gianni Degli Antoni discuss the intricacies of the throttle mechanism on the new racer. Exposed valve springs are visible above the exhaust port. Tartarini went on to establish his own company and build a variety of motorcycles under the Italjet label.

nearly a half-century passed before Mercedes revived the concept and employed it in its mighty, straight eight-cylinder racing engines. The Germans used no closing springs in the engine, relying on compression to push the valve the last few thousandths of an inch.

Without the resistance of valve springs to overcome, the desmo valvetrain was considerably more efficient. And by removing some 75 pounds of pressure forced against the cam, follower, and valve seat, the parts gained a longer lifespan. Power not lost to spring inertia was freed to propel the rear wheels; the Mercedes valvetrain could be rotated by hand, and the reduced friction boosted the engine's output by 30 horsepower. Velocette, Norton, and BMW had all explored the possibilities of desmodromic systems for motorcycles, but none appeared on production machines.

Small Racers

The 98-cc Marianna had performed well as a club racer, and the next step was the move to Gran Prix and the 125-cc double overhead-cam version of the Gran Sport. Ducati hired 14 riders to compete in all levels of national, European, and international competition, and

The 125 Gran Sport appeared as a prototype in 1955. With the 6-mm increase in bore and a 22-mm carburetor, the 125 was good for 12 horsepower at 9,800 rpm. Gianni Degli Antoni added more luster to the legend by winning the 125 class in the 1956 Milano-Taranto race. Tod Rafferty

Record-breaking performances were the most direct route to public recognition and motorcycle sales. In 1956 privateer riders Mario Carini and Santo Ciceri, with assistance from the factory, broke 46 world records at Monza with this Nardi streamlined 100-cc Gran Sport. Tod Rafferty

engine had dual overhead cams and made 16 horsepower at 11,500 rpm. These engines were used at the beginning of the 1956 racing season and revealed the persistent problem of valve float at high rpm. Enter the Desmo.

Desmodromic valve control had been successfully used in competition only on the Mercedes-Benz 300 SLR engines two years earlier and effectively disappeared when the German factory retired from racing in 1955. Taglioni had begun working on desmo valve control at Mondial in the 1940s. His system was distinguished by a third camshaft in the middle, geared to the opening cams, with rockers pulling the valves closed—no valve float, more lift, precise valve timing, a boost of some 3,000 rpm, and a nominal bump in horsepower.

The word *desmodromic* comes from two Greek words, *desmos,* a band or ligament, and *dromos,* a running race or race course. The runner's leg pushes off and pulls back—two positive motions. One of the first to experiment with desmodromic valves was A. F. Arnott, an Englishman who patented a design in 1910 that never reached production. The Delage Gran Prix engines of 1914 employed a desmo system with an auxiliary spring to close the valve near the end of its travel. Then,

1957: distribuzione desmo

Even as the records were falling, Taglioni was at work on a double overhead-cam 125 Grand Prix engine. With the twin cams, 25-mm carburetor, and 11:1 compression, the single was rated for 16 horsepower at 11,000 rpm. The next rendition would have desmodromic valves. Tod Rafferty

Franco Farné, shown here at Riccione in 1958, started at Ducati in 1951 and became the primary test rider. He worked closely with Taglioni, raced in nearly every form of motorcycle competition, and was involved in all racing development from Bologna for 50 years.

the desmo debuted at the Swedish GP in 1956. Although not on the world championship calendar that year, the race attracted a strong roster of privateers on Mondial and MV machines. The factory had done little track testing on the desmo engine and had not revealed it to the the press. They planned to use Sweden as the preliminary effort for a serious assault at the Italian Gran Prix a few weeks later. The engine featured a dual-plug head and 10:1 compression; ignition advance was 36 degrees.

But Bologna's apprehension proved unwarranted when test rider Gianni Degli Antoni not only won the event but lapped the entire field. The team's elation was leavened by a measure of embarrassment at how easy the victory had been, though Ducati immediately set to work on preparing for the Italian event. But three weeks later, misfortune struck with force when Antoni was killed in testing at Monza. The young racer had won the Milano-Taranto race in 1955 and was the factory's leading test rider. Antoni's death hit Taglioni hard and virtually disengaged the factory's international racing effort for a year.

The engineer did continue work on the valve system to achieve the close tolerances necessary for reliable performance, and on the bottom end to resolve weaknesses that had been exposed by the high rpm. By 1957 the Ducati team, on single overhead-cam 125-cc racers, dominated the major Italian endurance events such as the Motogiro and Milano-Taranto distance races. Giuliano Maoggi, Leopoldo Tartarini, Francesco Villa, and Bruno Spaggiari were national heroes, and Ducati dealerships were busy with customers. Taglioni worked concurrently on a 175-cc version of the single overhead-cam engine, and Franco Farne, who started with Ducati in 1951, became the leading development rider for the factory and competed in motocross and roadracing.

Bruno Spaggiari bought his first motorcycle, a Ducati Gran Sport, in 1955 and caught the racing bug. With Alberto Gandossi, he won the the 24 Hours of Montjuich (Barcelona) 125 class in 1957 and the Italian Gran Prix in 1958. At Montjuich in 1964, he and Giuseppe Mandolini won overall on a 285-cc Ducati. Spaggiari would ride with Ducati for nearly 20 years, with interludes aboard MV, Benelli, and Morini. Leo Tartarini would go on to design motorcycle chassis and found the Italjet company.

Another prominent racer was MV rider Luigi Taveri from Switzerland, who switched to Ducati in 1958 and came third in that year's 125-cc world championship. Taveri moved to Honda in 1961 and eventually won the 125-cc title three times.

The factory's decision to regroup in 1957 made a number of double overhead-cam 125 Grand Prix racers available to privateers. These later machines had a twin-tube cradle frame and were campaigned successfully throughout Europe and England in the late 1950s. Taglioni brought the 175-cc engine to life in the same chassis and had the 125 Desmo ready for the 1958 season. This time the Ducatis took the top five places in the Italian Gran Prix, certifying the functional value of Taglioni's desmodromic design and engraving Ducati Meccanica in the history books.

But for Gandossi's crash while leading the Irish Gran Prix, Ducati would have taken the world championship from MV. But it was MV's Ubbiali in the top spot, with Gandossi and Taveri second and third for Ducati. MV also won the 250 crown with Tarquinio Provini and Britain's John Surtees doubling in the 350- and 500-cc divisions.

Ducati's point proven, the company stepped away from Gran Prix racing in 1959 to develop the road models for a growing export market. Many of the desmo machines were converted to standard configuration and sold as production racers. The desmos and top shelf spares went to former members of the factory team, and to a motorcycle dealer from Great Britain named Stan

Hailwood. His son Michael had ridden a Ducati to tenth place in his first European Gran Prix at Assen in 1958. Advance word in the paddock was that young Michael was just a cheeky bloke from Oxford with a rich motorcycle dealer for a father. Nothing to worry about.

In 1959, Mike Hailwood won the Ulster Gran Prix and finished the season third in points in the 125 class, behind the MVs of Ubbiali and Provini, who also ended 1-2 in the 250-cc class. MV-mounted John Surtees

Mike Hailwood at 19 on the 125 Ducati twin. Although it revved to 14,000 rpm, the desmo twin had a skinny powerband and didn't handle very well. Plus, the complicated spur-gear cam drive was fragile. Later 250- and 350-cc versions proved no more satisfactory.

The production version of the dual overhead-cam Bialbero retained the single-downtube frame with an added twin-tube section below the engine. These were built as limited production racing machines for two years, proving quite successful for privateers throughout Europe. Tod Rafferty

A stylish one-piece cam box cover enclosed the 125 GP's collection of top-end gears. A limited number of 175-cc Bialbero engines were also made in 1959, and some of both engines were fitted to the twin-downtube cradle frame designed for the factory racing machines. Tod Rafferty

repeated his titles in the 350- and 500-cc classes. Hailwood also had two of the three 125-cc Desmo twins that Ducati had campaigned the year before. The twin was only marginally more powerful than the single, though it had a 10-mile per hour advantage on top speed. The twin would spin to 14,000 but was peaky and more difficult to ride consistently, and Hailwood switched at midseason to the single. At Hailwood's request, the factory built 250- and 350-cc versions of the twin, but their performance never met expectations.

125 Gran Sport

Ducati had since quit the Gran Prix scene to refine its road machines and develop a reliable international dealer network. Brothers Joseph and Michael Berliner had moved from their native Hungary to the United States in 1947. In New Jersey they established the Berliner Motor Corporation and became distributors for Jawa motorcycles from Czechoslovakia, later adding Germany's Zundapp and Sachs to the roster. But two-strokes had never gained wide popularity among American motorcyclists, and the Berliners sought to add a four-stroke to the mix. In 1958, at the annual Cologne

Hailwood

Michael Stanley Bailey Hailwood rode his first roadrace at England's Oulton Park in 1957, when he was 17. He finished 10th on a borrowed MV 125 and enjoyed it so much that, as he said later, "I decided to carry on." He would carry on to become the dominant Grand Prix rider of his generation, and arguably the best ever. His early success on Ducati motorcycles led to offers from Honda and MV in the larger-displacement classes, and he rode both to world championships. Twenty years later he came out of retirement to ride a Ducati V-twin to a thrilling victory at the Isle of Man. So Ducati's association with Mike Hailwood proved quite beneficial at critical points in the company's early and middle years.

His learning curve was short, and Hailwood went to the front quickly, winning seven British national titles in 1958 and 1959. His victories came aboard Paton, Mondial, NSU, Ducati, and Norton machines, so he could obviously win on any motorcycle brand. These feats didn't go unnoticed by Honda, which first came to the Isle of Man in 1959. Hailwood put his Norton Manx in third at the island in 1960, behind the MVs of Surtees and John Hartle. In 1961, shortly after his 21st birthday, Mike Hailwood won the 125- and 250-cc classes on Hondas, on the same day. Both of the Hondas were loaners, and Hailwood had put the factory riders, Jim Redman, Rob Phillis, and Luigi Taveri, behind him. He also won the Senior TT on Norton and had been leading the 350 class on an AJS when his engine broke 13 miles from the finish. Cheeky bloke indeed.

motorcycle trade show in Germany, they came across the Ducati 175.

Dr. Taglioni's first production bevel-drive, overhead-cam machine appeared in 1957 in sport and touring versions. These engines became the backbone of Ducati's export business and remained in production for 17 years with few significant changes aside from displacement. The Berliners reached an agreement with Dr. Montano to distribute Ducati motorcycles in the United States and placed an order for a shipment of 125- and 175-cc singles for 1959. A number of American dealers were also taken with the stylish little machines, and first-year sales tripled the factory's expectation. The following year saw an increase of 30 percent, more good news in Bologna and Jersey.

The Ducati singles got an enthusiastic reception from American sport riders, especially those familiar with their racing exploits in Europe. Lightweight sportbikes in the States had been largely limited to two-strokes (still widely perceived as unproven technology in the provinces) and some British pushrod singles without much grunt.

The motorcycle market worldwide was on the cusp of a phenomenal boom in popularity and sales, so Ducati was in the right place at the right time with what appeared to be the right products. Other forces would conspire to dilute the optimism that prevailed, but the Berliners and Ducati had established a strong foothold in the U.S. market when the 1960s arrived. No one at the time could have predicted the impact Honda would have on motorcyling worldwide, and Bologna would be hobbled by labor union rules imposed by the government administrators. Everyone was to have a job in Italy, regardless of ability, which led inevitably to economic chaos. In the 15 years following World War II, the Italian republic changed governments 22 times.

So the 1960s would see the re-introduction of two-strokes to the Ducati menu in an effort to gain some of the lightweight market. No license was required for mopeds in Italy. Development continued, however, on the overhead-cam singles, and once in a while Taglioni would look over another set of drawings in his desk outlining the design for a V-twin.

Only three of the 125-cc desmo twins were built, two of which went to Stan Hailwood in England. Young Michael gave it his best, but couldn't put the twin on the pace with the proven singles. In mid-1959 he went back to the single and won his first Grand Prix in Ireland.
Tod Rafferty

CHAPTER 3

Coming to America

1960-1970

A merican motorcyclists in the early 1960s were in the recreational minority, but one about to witness a rush of unprecedented growth in the numbers of both motorcycles and riders. Dozens of machines from Europe, England, and Japan were on display in showrooms throughout the country, with Harley-Davidson the remaining patriotic stalwart. Consider the menu: Ariel, BSA, Velocette, Triumph, Norton, AJS, Royal Enfield, Benelli, Cushman, Ducati, Zundapp, BMW, Sachs, NSU, Maico, Marusho, Honda, Yamaha, Suzuki, Kawasaki, Hodaka, Whizzer, Moto Guzzi, Matchless, Parilla, Aermacchi, Bridgestone, Bultaco, Ossa, Montesa, CZ, Jawa, Garelli, Motobic, DKW, Gilera, Greeves, James, Cotton, Dot, MZ, and Puch, to name the most. All told, more than 50 brands populated the scene.

Honda soon assumed leadership of this assembly, in terms of production capacity, new models, engineering, and sales figures. The Honda phenomenon of the mid-1960s actually worked to the benefit of most other manufacturers, at least in boosted sales for the short term, although Ducati dropped well to the back of the pack as the decade progressed. The Italian economy didn't enjoy anything near the health of the North American markets, and the Italian government-management machinery was slow to keep pace with the most recent moto-revolution. Also, the Italians were generally dubious about the long-term prospects of the American market.

The Mach 1 was widely admired for both its style and performance; this custom restoration by Todd Millar now resides in the Guy Webster collection. The factory also offered 250- and 350-cc S models in the twin-tube cradle frame, with larger brakes for endurance racing. The Mach 1 lasted until 1967. Guy Webster

The single overhead-cam series, 125- and 175-cc singles, began appearing in the United States in the late 1950s. Both were offered in sport and touring editions, and the 175S made 14 horsepower and better than 80 miles per hour. The 10-horse 125 Sport was distinctive in its blue-and-gold livery. Guy Webster

The 1960s were, nonetheless, successful years for Ducati in the United States. The Berliners established a national dealer network and helped nourish the growing faction of American riders drawn to what the Europeans called a cafe racer. The American renditions, most of them postwar Indians and Harleys, were called bobbers, alley racers, or street trackers—two-wheeled hot rods.

The two styles differed significantly in form and function. American street racers derived from large V-twins and emulated the look of dirt-track machines. The wide handlebars and upright seating position contrasted with the European roadracing crouch. Coming from distinctly different racing traditions, the two configurations had little in common. But European roadracing was gaining American adherents, although the American Motorcycle Association was not yet inclined to expand the national championship meets beyond three or four events per year.

With their marketing foothold in place, the Berliners reasoned that the next level had to include an expanded line of Ducati motorcycles. By 1962 the roster included the 125 Super, 175 Americano, and 250 Scrambler, Diana, and Monza. Taglioni's original 125 Sport had generated the 125 Monza, which was accompanied by a Super version with a nastier cam, more compression, and an unplugged exhaust system. This series begat the 175 Sport and 200 Elite renditions, which featured the

jello-mold fuel tank. The bevel-gear overhead-cam engines, in various stages of tune, were fitted to standard, touring, sport, and motocross models. British and American variants were given different names—the 175 Tourismo was the Americano in the States, with Harley-style buckhorn handlebars. This was the first signal of the Berliner effect in the Americanization of Ducati, which would be eclipsed in a few short years by the Hondafication of America.

Ducati also offered a stable of economy models, running the pushrod engines that had begun production as the Ducati 98 in 1952. The 98-cc and 125-cc version (called the Bronco in the States) had gear-drive primary and a four-speed transmission but only modest horsepower. The 125 Bronco's top speed was about 55 miles per hour, and the rather tall first gear required some clutch slippage to get under way. Relatively few of the pushrod-engines were brought to the United States, a market now coming quickly under the domination of the mini street and trail bikes from Honda.

The Berliners joined British distributor Stan Hailwood and others who were badgering Bologna for a 250-cc version to run against the singles from Triumph, BSA, Enfield, and the growing field of Japanese two- and four-strokes. Even though the factory racing effort had been discontinued, Ducati still turned out production

racing specials and spare parts for enthusiasts throughout Europe, Australia, and the United States. The 125 and 175 Formula 3 models were effectively purebred racing machines that shared few components with the road models. Although fitted with street-legal appointments, the bikes had sand-cast engine cases, straight-cut gears, and trick cams, pistons, transmissions, frames, and suspension components.

When Ducati management acceded to multiple requests for a 250, with stringent budgetary constraints attached, Taglioni produced an enlarged 175 that was good for 32 horsepower at 9,000 rpm. Like the 125 and 175 Formula Three, the 250 was built in limited numbers and was quite expensive for its class. In 1960, Ducati sent Francesco Villa, one of Italy's best roadracers, to the United States to demonstrate the 250's abil-

ities, and spectators came away suitably impressed. Ducati was on its way, well positioned in the gathering swell of international motorcycle marketing.

The timing was fortuitous. The 1960s ushered in a blossoming of amateur and professional competition in the United States; scrambles and flat track were flourishing, enduro and cross-country events attracted more entrants, and American roadracing tagged along as the fledgling stepson. Roadracing in the United States had never reached European levels of enthusiasm, and the next popular competition import to come Stateside in the 1960s would be motocross. Pavement racers were consequently relegated to sports car circuits, abandoned airports, and the Daytona Super Speedway.

American roadracers made the best of wildly disparate track conditions, having become accustomed to

The 175-cc Formula 3 racer was the dream of many a boy racer in 1958. Franco Farné was dispatched to the United States to demonstrate the racing capabilities of a small, light machine. Among the captivated was the young Phil Schilling, who still owns the example shown here.
Bruce Armstrong

The Bronco, in 85-, 98-, and 125-cc iterations, was developed from the original pushrod single. The entry-level bikes were also offered in touring (three-speed) and sport (four-speed) models. Berliner promoted the Americanized version with larger seat and high handlebars, but had little success. Bill McMillan

the hind teat tradition. Plus, at the professional level, there weren't that many of them. Cal Rayborn, Dick Mann, and Gary Nixon could run with the fastest European riders on a given day, but most of the Yanks were dirt-track specialists. So American roadracing, both pro and amateur, would remain on a slow growth curve for some years to come.

Ducati would be instrumental in the eventual growth of American roadracing and the cafe racer market, but the 1960s delivered some costly lessons on the riding preferences of Yankee customers. Indeed, the U.S. market proved to be considerably larger, and more multilayered, than most manufacturers ever dreamed. Bologna could not afford to keep a warehouse well stocked with spare parts, and management seemed to think it was doing well enough to get the motorcycles out the door. American riders and dealers soon began to register their displeasure with poor finish work, mystifying wiring systems, and fragile electrics that made Joseph Lucas seem a prince of illumination. The task at hand was, nonetheless, to supply the growing demand for motorcycles.

Stylish sportbikes alone could not provide the financial backbone to keep Ducati competitive in the 1960s,

so mopeds and scooters returned to the product line. The Brisk and Piuma mopeds employed a 48-cc two-stroke engine in a pressed-steel frame, while the sport version was given a tubular chassis. This model would beget a dual-purpose version called the Cacciatore in Europe and the Falcon in the United States. Next came the Super Falcon 80, an 80-cc version with 4.25 horsepower that was replaced by the 94-cc Cadet and Mountaineer models. Sales in the United States were not noteworthy.

The Brio scooter was also equipped with a two-stroke engine and was a far less elaborate construction than the previous Cruiser. In its second year, the Brio was expanded from 50- to 100-cc and exported to mostly other European countries. The engine was mounted to the swingarm, so chain tension was constant. The Brio was used for many years by the Bologna traffic police.

With the arrival of the 250-cc overhead-cam singles, Ducati registered its arrival as a player in the American market. *Cycle World* magazine was one of the first American publications to road test the new machines and presented the Scrambler in 1962. This 250 was one of the first multipurpose motorcycles to arrive from Europe, fitted with dirt-track style handlebar, trials-universal tires, sloped seat, and detachable headlight. Berliner offered an optional countershaft and rear sprockets, and struts to replace the shocks for flat track racing. With 9:1 compression, the 250 Scrambler engine was rated for 30 horsepower at 7,500 rpm and weighed 275 pounds with precious lubricating and combustible fluids aboard.

The magazine's testers were taken with the power and handling of the Scrambler and surprised by its acceleration and speed. With stock gearing, the four-speed 250 posted a top speed of 82 miles per hour, and it was apparent that the Scrambler was aimed directly at the hot rod heart of American riders. Not in the league with Harley's 55-horsepower Sportster maybe, but at $670 the Ducati was less than half the price and little more than half the weight.

By 1962 the international two-stroke revolution had reached showroom floors in the United States. Bultaco, Ossa, Montesa, Husqvarna, Maico, AJS, Greeves, Yamaha, Suzuki, Bridgestone, and others were represented, with machines that were generally faster, cheaper, and easier to maintain than a Ducati. Bologna's two-stroke roster was restricted to mopeds and small-bore sporties for schoolboy budgets, and Taglioni had little interest in valveless technology.

Singular Success

Cycle World technical editor Gordon Jennings tested the Ducati Diana Mark 3 in 1963 and described the performance as "quite impressive." He rated the Diana the "fastest, and nearly the smoothest, standard motorcycle in the 250-cc class. Moreover, it delivers performance without fussiness, and the example provided us for purposes of testing was returned to its owners after all excuses for keeping it longer had been exhausted—we liked it that much." Ray Hempstead won the Daytona 40-mile 250 Sportsman event on a Ducati that year, and Bill Varnes led the 20-mile Lightweight field home on his Ducati 125.

By 1964 the Diana Mark 3 had 10:1 compression, the flywheel magneto from the Scrambler, and five gears in the transmission. The carburetor size had dropped from 30 to 27 mm, broadening the power band, and the five-speed was 10 pounds lighter than its predecessor. *Cycle World* again extolled the bike's virtuous handling, rev-happy engine, aluminum brake drums, and overall Italian panache, cachet, and aural erotica when fitted with the racing megaphone. The testers admitted that

the Mark 3 was less suitable as a touring machine, given the firm seat and absence of a battery, and that the Monza would be preferable for road work of any distance. But that was the point of the Taglioni Ducatis after all, sportsman racers for the open road.

The European verson of the Mark 3 was the Mach 1, with a battery/coil ignition and slightly taller internal gearing. This was effectively the next iteration of the 175/250 F3 production racers, and the testbed for the ensuing generation of overhead-cam singles from Bologna. The Mach 1 and Mark 3 began to merge components in the mid-1960s, until the Mach 1 name was abandoned and the Mark 3, with battery and coil ignition, became the sport model for both domestic and export markets.

With the advent of the five-speed model, the *Cycle World* staff caught the roadracing bug, and Jennings set

Francesco Villa won the Formula Three event at Monza in 1958 on the factory 175, which underscored Spaggiari's 125 Grand Prix victory with the new desmo engine. In the United States, George Rockett and Sydney Tunstall put the 175 F3 in the winners' circle at club races. Bruce Armstrong

This 1958 175 Formula 3 has been restyled as a custom roadster. The 175 engine ran a 22.5-mm carburetor with 11:1 compression. The machine was offered with either a four- or five-speed gearbox, and made 21 horsepower at 10,500 rpm. Tod Rafferty

about bringing the Ducati's performance in line with the Yamaha TD-1 and Harley/Aermacchi CR Sprint. Jennings started with the head and completely reworked the intake port as a starting point.

"Somebody at Ducati thought that what you did was bring the port straight in at the valve, and the flow just won't make that turn. So I bored the port completely out of the head and welded in a stub. Then I put a Matchless intake valve in and moved the Ducati intake valve over to the exhaust side, which is a dangerous thing to do, because exhaust valves have to be stainless steel, or something that won't go off like a sparkler. But the Ducati used the same alloys in both valves.

"This is one of the projects that got me the nickname PiR Squared. Because rather than just cutting and hoping, I had gathered some literature from the better engine builders, and I knew what kinds of gas speeds I was looking for in the port. C. R. Axtell got engines to run hard by dint of experience and endless work. I looked for ways to regularize the whole thing, to make it all make a little sense. This thing had valves and ports that conformed with the engines built by Wally Hassett at Coventry-Climax."

Jennings was assisted in the project by racer Frankie Scurria, who had won the 1964 AAMRR Sebring race on a Manx Norton. "Frankie was pretty fast on a motorcycle, and he was a completely engaging character and always up to something absolutely mad. He broke his leg badly, the second time, at Daytona in 1965 where I found him rolling around in front of my front wheel.

"He smashed the leg badly enough that they were going to amputate it, and he said nothing doing, just splint it and send me back to California. When he got back the real doctors, orthopedic surgeons, patched him up. But he didn't race motorcycles anymore; he did race cars."

The *Cycle World* project racer made better than 30 real horsepower (the stocker made 22 on the dyno), spun to 11,000 rpm, and weighed 233 pounds with a fairing. The 29-mm Dell'Orto carburetor was replaced by a 1 3/8-inch Amal GP mixer, and the Ducati ignition gave way to a Stefa magneto for more reliable high-rpm spark. After some success, the bike was sold to local racer Ralph LeClercq.

"I have to admit that I had very little faith in that Ducati," says Jennings, "so I was perfectly happy to see it sold to Ralph, who'd been racing a 175 Ducati. Then I was at Willow Springs on my spiffy new 'real racer' Aermacchi 250, right in a Yamaha TD1's draft coming up the front straight. I thought I was in pretty good shape if the Sprint would run with a TD1, even in the draft, then I wasn't too far out of it. Then Ralph LeClercq came by on that 250 Ducati and passed both of us."

At six-feet-one, Jennings was a tad large for the smaller racing machines like the Ducati. "When I started racing I weighed about 185. Then when I started getting

Taglioni's original Gran Sport engine came to refinement in the 175-cc single overhead-cam single, the foundation for decades of Ducatis to come. The design soon spawned 250-, 350-, and 450-cc versions in street, roadracing, and dirt bike trim. It would eventually double itself as a 750-cc V-twin.

serious I began to peel weight off myself; because there's no point in drilling holes in things on the motorcycle and using titanium bits if you have a butt so big that you have to sit down in shifts. Or, as somebody said, if they tell you to haul ass and you have to make two trips. I dieted myself down to 156 pounds and looked like a concentration camp survivor, and had no strength at all. I had to get back to about 163. Nature did not have motorcycle racing in mind when I was designed.

"What I remember best about Italian motorcycles of that period was that the seats seemed to be designed either by someone who had never seen a human ass, or that they had seen one and decided to give every motorcyclist a wedgie. Truth to tell, I was not really that fond of any of the Ducatis of that period. The 250 was a spirited little thing and would run hard, but it was still a 250. Notwithstanding the racer I built at *Cycle World,* I didn't get really interested in Ducatis until the V-twin came along."

The Berliner Declension

By 1963 the strength of the American motorcycle market had conferred upon the Berliners a greater measure of managerial influence in Bologna. The Italians were still uncertain what to make of the American distributors, or the curious styling they favored, but sales figures were up in the States and down in the domestic market. This New Jersey leverage extended to the design and engineering of the motorcycles, and would be responsible for the 160 Monza Junior, 350 and 450 Street Scramblers, and the 1,257-cc Apollo V-4.

The Apollo was an attempt by Berliner to contest Harley-Davidson's dominance of the U.S. police bike market, a lucrative—and high-profile—segment for any manufacturer. The Apollo was, especially for an Italian motorcycle, a genuine behemoth. The 90 V-4, rated for 60 horsepower at 6,000 rpm, was housed in a combined box-section and tubular frame and weighed 630 pounds.

The pushrod overhead-valve engine featured four 24-mm Dell'Orto carburetors, gear-drive primary, and a four-speed transmission, with a starter motor lifted from a Fiat 1100. The 5.00x16 Pirelli tires were unhappy with the combined power and weight of the Apollo mission, and registered their disapproval by shredding their treads. So the engine was detuned for less power, which made the overall weight a larger performance handicap. The Apollo never reached production, although it provided Taglioni some lessons for the eventual design of the V-twin.

Berliner also instituted the development of a 500-

cc parallel twin, which would be displayed with the Apollo at the Daytona Beach motorcycle show in 1965. Also a pushrod overhead-valve engine, the twin featured a five-speed transmission and electric starter. Development work on the twin continued for several years, but it also never reached production.

By the mid-1960s, Ducati found itself in the role of a solitary David facing a platoon of Goliaths. The contest between Honda and Yamaha for racing superiority had raised performance levels (read *horsepower*) considerably. Harley-Davidson's partnership with Aermacchi had produced an upgraded 250-cc pushrod single that made 33 horsepower at 10,000 rpm, and the British industry was scrambling to keep up in the American market. Yamaha and Suzuki were enjoying a healthy business in two-stroke street and trail machines, and European two-strokes were at the forefront of the worldwide boom in motocross bikes. And with the Honda Hawk and Super Hawk drawing more attention from sporting riders, Ducati was confronted with seriously strong competition. The Berliner-induced model machinations showed few signs of reversing the situation.

The ascendence of the Japanese motorcycle industry in the 1960s has been well documented, usually in

The 1958 Elite 200 was among the first Ducatis exported in numbers to the United States. The stylish single was offered as the high-handlebar America or the sporty Elite SS shown here. The Super Sport was absent the road model's redundant dual muffler, and had flat bars and smaller fenders. Guy Webster

DUCATI

200 élite

MOTO DUCATI

4 stroke

200 cc.

Timing by O.H.C.

Gearbox 4 speeds.

Maximum speed Km/h 135 (Ml/h 83.534).

Fuel consumption lt. 3.4 per 100 Kms (81 Ml/imp. gal. = 69 Ml/US gal.).

MOTORCYCLE

ENGINE - Single-cylinder - Bore: 67 mm. - Stroke 57.8 mm. - Displacement 203.783 cc. - Compression ratio: 7.8 : 1 - Timing by O.H.C. valves inclined 80° - Maximum output: HP 18 - Maximum revs. per minute 7,500 - Cooling by air - Lubrication: forced by gear pump - Oil sump in crankcase - Ignition by distributor - Sparking plug: Marelli CW 260 N - Electrical equipment: Battery fed - Battery recharged by means of an alternator-flywheel and rectifier - Three-light headlamp - Tail light with Stop - Horn - Transmission: from engine to gearbox, by gears; from gearbox to wheel, by chain with special cushion drive - Gearbox: in unit with engine - 4 speeds; gears in constant mesh; pedal control with preselector - Clutch: multiplate discs running in bath of oil.

FRAME - Highly resistant steel tubing. Built on smart lines - Front suspension: telehydraulic fork complete with steering dampers - Rear suspension: swinging fork with adjustable hydraulic shock absorbers - Wheels: spoke type; chromium steel rims with special Sport profile; 18" × 2¼" - Brakes: expanding; front, hand operated; rear, brake foot - Drum diameter: front, 180 mm.; rear, 160 mm. - Tyres: 2,75-18; front, ribbed; 3,00-18 with block tread, the rear.

Weight (unladen) . . . . . . Kg. 111 (lbs. 244.710)
Oil sump holds approx . . . Kg. 2 (lt. 2.400 = lbs. 4.409)
Fuel tank holds . . . . lt. 17 (imp. gal. 3.3796 = US gal. 4.4909)

DUCATI MECCANICA S.p.A. - P.O.B. 313 - PHONE: 49.16.01 - BOLOGNA (ITALY)

STUDIO LUCY   LITOGRAFIA SCARANI - BOLOGNA   PRINTED IN ITALY

The 200 Elite, distinguished by its twin Silentium mufflers and morphic fuel tank, was originally based on the 175. Later models used downsized versions of the 250 engine, and were sold in SS and GT renditions. The Elite was superseded by the 250 models, and was last produced in 1965.

terms of sterling engineering, production efficiency, astute management, and Honda's sociological role in making motorcycles more popular in the United States. Often overlooked is the fact that Honda and Yamaha both followed the Ducati (or Italian) formula in achieving racing success first, then moving to production motorcycles. Luigi Taveri, who finished third in the 125-cc world championship on a Ducati in 1958, took the same spot in 1961 on a Honda 125 and became world champion on Honda in 1962, 1964, and 1966. Mike Hailwood, who won his first Grand Prix in 1959 on Ducati, won the 250-cc championship for Honda in 1961.

Ducati had established an agreement with Mototrans of Barcelona to manufacture Spanish models under license in the late 1950s. The company specialized in two-stroke machines, competing against Montesa, Ossa, and Bultaco in Spain, where sportbike mania is at least equal to if not greater than it is in Italy. Mototrans built its own 250- and 350-cc versions of the ill-fated Ducati inline four, but only prototypes were developed. A non-desmo with 16 valves, the four appeared in 1965 but was soon shelved.

However, Mototrans/Ducati singles were quite successful in national races and in the Barcelona 24-hour race at Montjuich Park. Quality control on production machines was not always up to the Bologna factory standards, but Mototrans' products cost considerably less in Spain than the import duty–laden Italian models.

European roadracing did begin showing some influence in the United States by the mid-1960s. In 1963, the first year fairings were permitted by the American Motorcycle Association (AMA), Ducatis were well represented at Daytona. In the first combined expert/amateur/novice 250 event, Jim Hayes put his Ducati third behind the Honda of Jess Thomas and winner Dick Hammer's Harley/Aermacchi Sprint. Ray Hempstead and Bill Varnes, both Ducati-mounted, won the 250 and 125 sportsman classes respectively.

Most of the other American pavement races were club events at the amateur level, but the AMA's long-standing refusal to affiliate with Europe's Federation Internationale Motocycliste (FIM) created a few racing options. One of the most active alternatives was the American Association of Motorcycle Road Racers (AAMRR) in the East, which held races under FIM rules at such tracks as Watkins Glen and Bridgehampton, New York; Summit Point and Danville, Virginia; Nelson Ledges, Ohio; and Sebring, Florida. The AAMRR, more commonly know as

the Alphabet Racers, did associate with the FIM and honored European and Canadian racing licenses. The American Cycle Association (ACA) and American Federation of Motorcyclists (AFM) did likewise on the West Coast.

At its final event of 1964 at Watkins Glen, the AAMRR drew an entry roster of 132 riders. Among them was British expatriate Ian Gunn with a Ducati 200 Elite and new five-speed 250 Mach 1/S in the junior class, and expert George Rockett on a 175 F3, 250 and 350 Ducati factory specials, and Norton 500.

Gunn won the 250 junior class, his first roadracing victory, and Rockett was first in the 175 and 350, fourth in the 500 class, and won the Unlimited division on the Norton.

Ian Gunn saw his first Ducati in 1959, at the Palomar Observatory in California. "This little Italian bike was sitting there in the parking lot. It was a fascinating design, and I'd never even heard of one before. I thought it was beautifully designed, and I've been a Ducati enthusiast ever since." Gunn, who at age 71 occasionally races a Ducati 888, and still has his 200 Elite and 250 Mach 1/S. He also owns an ex-Hailwood desmo 125 (three-cam) twin and two-cam 175 twin, plus a 750 SS and numerous other motorcycles.

"The Mach 1 I basically raced into the ground," Gunn says. "It was quite competitive for a long time;

then its crankpin broke at Mosport. It's a problem I've seen on other Ducatis; the finishing grind in the bore in the flywheels, where the crankpin presses in, they didn't clean up the roughing cut. The Mach 1/S has a slightly different flywheel, the rod and pin are a little heavier, and the big end bearing was special too."

The 125 Desmo twin, one of three made, was rated for 22 horsepower at 14,000 rpm. But Gunn was only able to see 12,000 at Summit Point, and the ignition and valve timing checked out true. "But it had a couple cast pistons with very wide rings, and I'm pretty sure it was suffering from ring flutter. But I have two new forged pistons, a stack of 1 mm-wide rings, and several unused cylinder sleeves."

The 175 twin was built for the Italian long-distance events at the request of Leo Tartarini, who went on to establish Italjet. "I've never run it yet," said Gunn. "It's on the list to do after I get the 125 running." Ian distinguished himself in the 1960s at Vineland, New Jersey, by proving that a Ducati single, toolbox, cooler, and small passenger could be transported in a Volkswagen Beetle.

In 1965 the American Motorcycle Association schedule held a record-setting seven national championship roadraces. The motorcyclists' annual pilgrimage to Daytona took on new dimensions, with an FIM inter-

national Grand Prix at the Speedway, followed by Alphabet races at Sebring, and then the AMA 200-miler. This was the second year that motorcycles ran on the Daytona banking, the first time on a rain-soaked track, and Harley's Roger Reiman won it convincingly.

A week earlier, Mike Hailwood (MV) again won the MICUS/FIM Grand Prix, lapping second place Buddy Parriot's Norton just past the halfway mark. Parriot went on to win the AAMRR/FIM race at Sebring, where Franco Farne won the 350 class for Ducati and finished 10th overall. The Ducatis of Richard Arden and John McCarthy topped the 200 and 175 classes respectively.

One of the AMA roadraces in 1965 was a 250-cc national at Nelson Ledges, a tight and nasty little circuit in the cornfields of northeastern Ohio. Dick Mann, 1963 National Champion, won the race on a Yamaha twin. Mann had also won the 250 class at Daytona, marking the first victory for a Japanese motorcycle in AMA Grand National competition. The advance scouts in the gathering two-stroke invasion now drew more attention from U.S. racers. Ducati riders searched for more power.

In 1966, Berliner presented the new five-speed Ducati 250 Scrambler as an all-purpose machine for the road, trail, and racetrack. The sporty single came equipped with a magneto ignition and straight exhaust pipe, and a standard equipment package that included three rear sprockets, an extra countershaft sprocket, and a cable set. In addition, the kit still included solid struts to replace the rear shocks for dirt-track racing, and a nominal muffler for the street. The shock springs were softer than the previous year's, in response to complaints about too-stiff suspension, and the fork had been strengthened via a welded, rather than pinned, lower triple clamp.

The 160 Monza Junior, an enlarged 125 engine in the 250 Monza chassis, signaled another Berliner variation for American motorcyclists. The styling, squared and angular, was not well received in the States or elsewhere and sales of the new model were minimal. The new look had also been adopted for the 250 Monza and 350 Sebring, in the apparent certainty that this "modern" style would captivate American riders. Berliner had invested heavily in the new models, and the results proved crippling for both the distributor and the Ducati factory. The combined failures of the Apollo, the 500-cc vertical twin, and the restyled models, exacerbated by the Honda effect, put Berliner in grievous financial straits.

Within three years, Berliner had plunged from its position as the second largest distributor of motorcycles

The Mach 1 appeared to rousing huzzahs from fans of lightweight sport bikes. A distilled edition of the Mark 3, the roadster was the boy racer to have in the mid-1960s. In a growing sea of fast Bultacos, Yamahas, and Suzukis, the Ducati remained the four-stroke stalwart. Guy Webster

The Apollo 90-degree V-4 engine had a bore and stroke of 84.5 x 56 mm for 1,257-cc. With compression at 8:1, and four 24-mm Dell'Orto carburetors, the big four had 80 rated horsepower at 6,000 rpm. Conceived as a Harley-fighter and police special, the Apollo never made it into production. Tod Rafferty

Among the most popular of the Ducati singles, the 250 Scrambler made the transition from the early four- and five-speed narrow-case versions to the wide-case series in 1968. With the passage of years, the Scrambler became less dirt-oriented and adopted the dual-purpose/street scrambler demeanor.

in the United States to near the bottom of the barrel. The New Jersey firm was also the Stateside agent for Associated Motor Cycles (AMC) of England, manufacturers of Norton, Matchless, and AJS machines. In 1967, unable to pay for a shipment of 3,400 Ducatis, Berliner notified AMC that importation of its motorcycles would be suspended until the Ducatis had been disposed of. The news caused something of a stir in Plumstead, East London. AMC, itself no picture of prosperity, could scarcely afford to suddenly be cut off from the American market, or to undertake the search for a new distributor.

Months went by as the British firm scrambled to find someone willing and able to take delivery of some $1.5 million worth of motorcycles. Finally an agreement was reached between bankers and Liverpool car dealer Bill Hannah to purchase the entire Ducati shipment. The deal alleviated the problem between AMC and Berliner, but inflicted serious damage to the relationship between Vic Camp, then the licensed Ducati distributor in England, and the Bologna factory. Nor had it done much for Berliner's standing with Ducati, which had been eroding since the expensive diversions of the Apollo and vertical twin. Nonetheless, Berliner would remain the American distributor for another 15 years.

Wider Is Better

Ducati was in no shape to establish a relationship with a new distributor in the States, even in the unlikely event that one could be found. Japanese motorcycles dominated the U.S. market; the British motorcycle industry was entering its closing chapter, and even the venerable Harley-Davidson Motor Company was up for bids.

Ducati managing director Giuseppe Montano resigned, and the Bologna factory was again under direct control of a government holding company. On the plus side, a new generation of improved overhead-cam singles was about to appear, and these would include the first production models with desmodromic valve gear. Also, at the corner of Fabio Taglioni's drawing table was the design for a 500-cc, 90-degree V-twin—a racing engine.

Product development in the European fashion rarely included completely new model designs. The second-generation Ducati singles, which came to be called wide-case engines for their wider-spaced engine mountings, were refined and strengthened versions of Taglioni's original design.

The updated renditions, intended as reinforcements against the overwhelming force of the Japanese manufacturers, incorporated better main bearings, connecting rods, stronger kickstarter gears, and larger crankpins. Oil capacity increased with a larger sump, and the new frame employed double downtubes at the rear. With the additional stoutness came a corresponding rise in the models' weight, which ensured the continuing popularity of the older narrow-case machines for production racing.

With its most recent reorganization, Ducati had received a substantial injection of lira from the Italian government, which was intent on maintaining employment levels in a still-shaky economy. Most of the costs for upgrading the singles had been derived from the previous budget, so the new funds allowed Ducati to develop something that might trump Japan's technology: production desmo heads.

The first wide-case model to reach the States was the 350 SSS (Street/Sports Scrambler), another Bolognese variation on the all-purpose motorcycle. Honda had effectively proven the efficacy of four-stroke street/dirt bikes, but its offerings consisted of heavy twin-cylinder adaptations of its street models. At the other extreme, the genuine off-road/enduro/motocross riders had largely heeded the ringing call of the two-stroke engine. So there appeared to be room in the middle ground for dual-purpose, single-cylinder, four-stroke motorcycles on the farm or ranch, in the mountains or desert, and in the suburbs among students and wannabe racers on a tight budget.

While the Ducati was demographically correct, Honda and Yamaha were upping the stakes by frequent leaps and bounds. The Yamaha DT1 was leading legions of adventurous folks off into the dirt trails, with increasing reliability. Although heavy, the Honda 305 and later 350 and 450 Scramblers were powerful, dependable, and had 12-volt electrical systems and pushbutton starters. The kickstart Ducati SSS still had a feeble, 6-volt electrical system.

In its favor, the 350 SSS weighed little more than 300 pounds, would pull to about 90 miles per hour, and featured distinctive Italian styling and well-engineered mechanicals. Rubber gaiters were fitted to both the fork tubes and shock absorbers. In 1969 the bike switched to a square-slide Dell'Orto with a new side-mount air cleaner. The 450 Scrambler appeared the same year, labeled the Jupiter in the United States. The 450 had new cases, cylinder, and head, and the frame was reinforced at the steering head.

Throughout the 1960s, Ducati continued to turn out limited runs of specialized roadracers for European

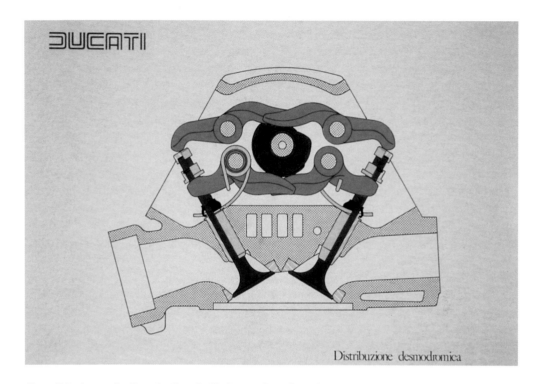

Distribuzione desmodromica

How things work: the single-shaft desmodromic valve system is elegantly simple and precisely efficient, though proper adjustment is critical. The upper set of rockers follow the opening lobes; the lower pair ride the closing cams. Taglioni's desmo design reached production Ducatis in 1968.

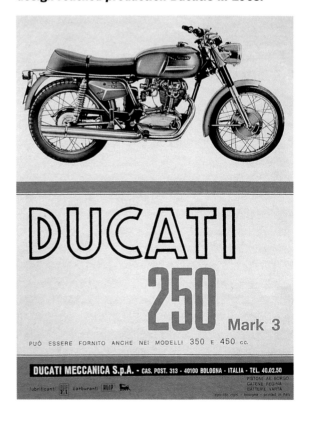

The 250 Mark 3 was the first Ducati to attract serious attention from lightweight enthusiasts in the United States. Fitted with a megaphone, it ran 104 mph and sold for under $700 in 1962.

With the arrival of the wide-case engines came the first production desmos. The 350 Mark 3D came to be widely regarded as the best balance of power and handling ever produced in Bologna. The 1968 model was distinguished by its dual fuel-filler caps, a one-year-only feature. Guy Webster

The first wide-case racers appeared in 1967, ridden by Roberto Gallina and Gilberto Parlotti. The desmo soon grew to 436-cc, developed by Farne's Scuderia Speedy Gonzales and piloted by Bruno Spaggiari. This example is fitted with a Ceriani suspension and 230-mm Fontana front brake.
Tod Rafferty

In 1969 the fuel tank had a single filler. Both horses and winged creatures have symbolized several Italian marques, with imagery tracing back to Roman mythology. Mercury (winged foot) was messenger of the gods, and also the god of commerce, manual skill, eloquence, cleverness, travel, and thievery.
Tod Rafferty

privateers and/or friends of the factory. Factory development rider Franco Farne had raced a prototype desmo 250 at Modena in 1966, with the Mach 1 engine as its foundation. The first wide-case 350 desmo was run in 1967, and Ducati provided Berliner with four each of the 250- and 350-cc machines for Daytona. Officials of the AMA refused the entries, citing the nonstandard forks and desmo heads as a "change in basic design." Technically true, probably, but Ducati had simply gotten too far ahead in its cheating, or too careless in disguising it. In any case, the Italian single would have gained little ground on the tuned Yamaha twins (now up to 135 miles per hour), even though the peak horsepressures were not so far apart. The Yamaha spooled its portion up much more quickly, but on a tight road course the Ducati displayed its better handling.

The single-camshaft 350 Desmo production engine was installed in the Mark 3 in the fall of 1968, followed shortly by 250 and 450 iterations. Another 500-cc pushrod parallel twin prototype was displayed for the press, but no production plans followed. The only visual differences between the desmo and standard machines were the letter *D* on the side panels and the word *DESMO* cast into the cam bearing plate. With a megaphone, the 350 delivered better than 30 horsepower and top speeds above 110 miles per hour. Quarter-mile times were in the low 15s.

Bruno Spaggiari was outfitted with a 450 Desmo in a gusseted frame with a reinforced swingarm, Ceriani fork, Amadoro racing drum brakes, and aluminum rims. With a 42-mm carburetor, the 450 pumped up more than 40 horsepower and produced top speeds above 120 miles per hour.

But plans for a street-legal replica were scrapped in favor of the off-road 450 R/T, developed for the scrambler-happy American market. The 250 and 350 Desmos continued to pester the Yamaha two-strokes and the British four-stroke 500 singles and twins in European roadracing. The nimble Ducatis, capable of higher entry and cornering speeds, were disadvantaged only on the long straights. In 1969, Britons A. M. Rogers and Charles Mortimer were first and third on Ducatis in the Isle of Man 250 Production race, and Mortimer won on a Mark 3 in 1970. The victory would register Ducati's last on the island until 1978, and the return to glory of Hailwood.

The Dell'Orto SS carburetor was supplanted in 1969 by the square-slide VHB model, less prone to wear, and the tapered Silentium muffler was replaced by a cut-off version in the American hot rod style. The 250/350/450 Mark 3 models came to the United States in 1970 in both standard and desmo versions. The engines were identical but for the desmodromic heads,

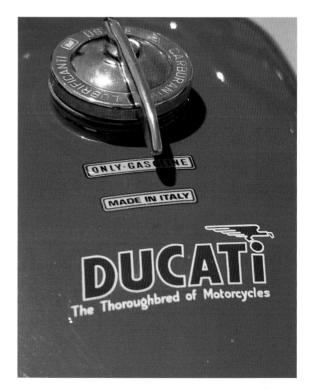

In 1971 the 250/350/450 Desmos were awarded the heavy-gauge silver metalflake paint scheme, which would generate the "Silver Shotgun" nickname. Guy Webster's 350D displays the new cafe racer livery, which included rearset controls, Borrani rims, and a Marzocchi racing fork. Guy Webster

and performance in stock trim was roughly equal. Racers could obtain a competition kit with a hotter cam, megaphone, jet selection, and fairing.

During a 1969 *Cycle* magazine road test, staffers swapped the stock muffler for a megaphone on the 350 Desmo. The result was a 2.5-second drop in quarter-mile times and 9-mile per hour boost on the top end. Unplugged, the 350 sprinted the quarter in 15.15 seconds, and with room to roll topped out at 112 miles per hour.

The Ducati singles would soon yield to the new V-twin, but the one-lung wonders held their popularity in Europe on into the 1980s. Mototrans, the Spanish licensee in Barcelona, kept the singles in production for years, and most of its machines were narrow-case four-speed models based on the original 175 engine of the 1950s. The Spaniards maintained an active racing department, with considerable support from Bologna, and brought many improvements to the marque. The factory posted numerous victories in the famed 24 Hours of Barcelona, run on the demanding hillside streets of Montjuich Park.

Sport riders and racers worldwide embraced the Ducati singles in the 1960s. Those accustomed to heavier twins and larger-displacement singles were impressed with the bike's stability and sharp handling; the engine's smoothness at high rpm felt more like a twin, and the

positive gear change offered added confidence. The skilled rider on a Ducati could delight in the exhilaration of rushing into turns much more quickly than a larger motorcycle would permit, or dear prudence would even dictate. And although the singles were eclipsed in the 1970s by the Ducati V-twin, they remained close to the hearts of lightweight enthusiasts everywhere, and are still winning in vintage events around the world.

Sittin' on the walk of the bay. The author's '68 350 Desmo was primary transportation around San Francisco in the mid-1970s, and was well–suited to the task.

CHAPTER 4

The Bevel V-Twins

1970-1983

By 1970 the crest of the motorcycle sales boom had passed, but the U.S. market remained strong and Honda was still on the top shelf. Ducati had introduced the Mark 3 Desmos (250/350/450) in 1969, with all three models available in standard valve-spring configuration as well. The 450 Scrambler had achieved market success in both Europe and the States, and the desmo version was expected to offer a four-stroke alternative to the pukka off-road market dominated by Japanese two-strokes. Its frame also provided a glimpse of what future Ducati chassis would look like, with its large-diameter steering head with tapered roller bearings and reinforced, multiple-tube backbone.

In Bologna, Taglioni was at work on a 500-cc 90 V-twin racing engine and a 750-cc production motor. The 500 began with bevel-drive, single overhead-cam heads, but eventually evolved to include belt-driven, double overhead desmodromic cams. This last had limited racing success but formed the basis for the later Pantah engines. Several frame layouts were tested, including one designed by Colin Seeley of England, which formed the pattern for the 750 chassis. The prototype 750 GT appeared in the summer of 1970, fitted with a Fontana four-leading-shoe front brake and center-axle fork. The production version came out the following summer, with a single Lockheed disc and leading-axle Marzocchi fork. The Dell'Orto carburetors on the pre-

Neo-classic/romantic Italian moto-architecture is distinguished by its clarity of line. The components, mechanical and otherwise, are rendered to unify the entire form. The harmony of design and function (going fast beautifully) gave Ducati the image of speed, handling, and style it was after. Bruce Finlayson

Crovario, Ducati 250 - v1.150; 8. Polo-S-Polo Cavalieri, 250, Tintinono Virgilio, Ducati Pisano, Ducati 250 - 2/6, Sassi-Superga, 250, Cresta Giovanni, Ducati 250 - 6/6. Valle Benedetto, 500, Marchetti Piñero, Ducati 450 - 2/6, Certaldo-Gambassi, 250; Vergato-Cereta, Sciloce, Padrini-Migheri, Ducati... 250 - 1975, Nutchino-Cima, 350; Curlo Luigi, Ducati 250 - Fuoristrada - Grosseto 250, Luigi Ciacchi, Ducati 250 - 2/6, Treviso, 500, Cocchi Adriano, Marchetti Piñero, Ducati 250 - 2/6, Certaldo-Gambassi, 500; Marchetti Piñero, Ettore, Ducati... Compionato Romano d'inverno, Oltre 250, Marzucci Roberto, Ducati 250 - 8/3, Ducati 450 - 29/6, Signorino-Collina Piottoiese, 250; Toracca Armando, Ducati 250 - Ducati 450 - 2/6, Certaldo-Gambassi, Sidecap, Pedrini-Migheri, Ducati 750 - 11/6; Giro Bassa Sabina, 250; Barbieri Danilo, Ducati 250 - 8/2, Giro Bassa Sabina, Oltre 22/8; Poggibonsi-Castellina, 250, Brettoni Augusto, Ducati 250 - 5/9, Isola Lin- Vergato-Cereta, 500, Lattieri Mario, Ducati 450 - 29/6, Figline Valdarno-4 Strade; AUSTRIA

The factory 500 GP bike of 1971 as ridden by Bruno Spaggiari.

production model were replaced by Amal concentrics and the engine was rated for 60 horsepower at 8,000 rpm at 8.5:1 compression. Road ready, the production 750 GT weighed 450 pounds.

Taglioni had, in a relatively short time, successfully doubled the Ducati single and created a singularly smooth 90-degree V-twin. Finning on the front cylinder ran horizontally to improve cooling, with the engine rotated rearward to shorten the wheelbase of the Seeley-style tubular frame. The single's hairpin valve springs were gone, replaced by coils, but the overhead cams were still driven by helical gears at both ends of the towershafts. The one-piece rods were carried side-by-side on caged roller bearings on the pressed together crankshaft, which rode on large ball bearings. The bore and stroke of 80 x 74 mm was nearly the same as the 350 single's.

The chrome-moly tubular steel frame looked a bit spindly against the long engine, but by using the engine as a stressed member, it was in fact plenty strong for the power and weight of the 750 GT. The double front down-tubes had a center brace and were bracketed by twin upper tubes at the steering head and bolted firmly to the engine crankcases at the bottom. A third center tube ran from the top of the steering head to two crossbraces between the horizontal tubes above the rear cylinder. The engine, swingarm, and centerstand bolted to large plates at the rear, and the chain adjusters were housed inside the swingarm tubes.

A single 11-inch Lockheed disc brake was fitted to the left Marzocchi fork slider, with bosses provided on the right leg to mount another disc. The single-leading-shoe Grimeca drum (very early models had a twin-leading-shoe) handled braking at the rear wheel, suspended by Marzocchi shock absorbers with three-position spring adjustment. The GT's 60-inch wheelbase reflected the length of the V-twin engine, and imposed characteristically slow steering on the extended chassis. Although the Ducati resisted being flicked into sharp bends like a single, it rewarded the pilot with assuring stability in high-speed sweepers. Most riders could live with the trade-off, and those with above-average abilities appre-

44

ciated the overall package with its low center of gravity, good brakes, and light weight.

In 1972, *Cycle* magazine chided Ducati for the mediocre detail work on the 750 GT, and the shabby fiberglass and funky switchgear. But the review concluded thus: "This year Ducati 750s will be in relatively short supply. So if you buy a motorcycle for the way it looks, or for its candy-apple paint scheme, or even for what it says about your manhood, then pass the Ducati 750 by and get something else. Let some down-to-the-marrow enthusiast buy the Ducati 750, some guy who wants the big V-twin because he knows—and appreciates—that as a mechanical thing, as a piece of machinery, as a motorcycle, the Ducati 750 really works."

Not everyone, however, was smitten with the twin's engine or the motorcycle's overall appearance. Compared to traditional V-twins the front cylinder was a visual oddity, poking forward through the frame, and some found the entire engine visually unappealing—even ugly. But others immediately added a space beside other hallmark V-twins—the Harley-Davidson Knuckle-head, and Vincent Black Shadow—for a new benchmark of engineering and design.

Taglioni's V-twin may have had its genesis in the single, but the 750 outstripped its predecessors in every way. The twin's perfect primary balance delivered a smooth, seamless flow of torque on demand, while the long chassis and good ground clearance graced the rider with confidence in long, high-speed curves. Only the Norton Commando could approach the Ducati for broad-band power, superb road manners, and rider security, at least among production motorcycles of the early 1970s.

The 750 GT was configured as a Grand Touring model, an automobile term that would later evolve as Sport Touring in motorcycle nomenclature. (Following other Euro-car letter designations, motorcycle makers adopted S [sport], SS [supersport], and T [touring] categories.) The European edition was fitted with clip-on or clubman handlebars, while the American model came with wider and higher bars with more pullback. This begged the question, from road burners and track racers alike, where is the sport model? It was, in fact, not far behind.

Two years later, the 750 Sport became a seminal motorcyle for Ducati. The mobile metal sculpture of one man, Fabio Taglioni, and a dedicated supporting cast of craftsmen, the Sport was the centerstone in Bolognese sportbike sensibility, setting the stage not merely for the high-performance 750 SS, but for Ducati's future. The GT was dressed as the gentleman tourer, its engine

Psychedelic posters survived into the 1970s. The 450 RT Desmo was Ducati's final rendition of a purpose-built dirt machine, with no concessions to street use. The stronger frame carried a 35-mm Marzocchi MX fork, with a 21-inch front wheel and plastic fenders.

The 750 GT first appeared in 1971. Bruce Finlayson's restored 1974 has been lightly modified in both form and function, with Sport pistons and 32-mm carburetors. The 750 GT claimed a good share of the sport-touring market that BSA/Triumph and Norton were in the process of departing. Bruce Finlayson

mildly tuned; the Super Sport would soon be along to serve the discriminating racer, on the road or track. Not nearly as popular then as the GT nor as coveted now as the SS, the Sport stood in the middle, a machine for the core group of those afflicted with acute Ducatism, the back road warriors and weekend canyon scratchers with limited recreational budgets.

Meanwhile, Triumph's new models were a disastrous departure from tradition, BSA was in its death throes, and Harley-Davidson was beginning to show the fractures of its corporate merger with AMF. Honda, however, had rocked and rolled the motorcycle world with the CB750 Four. Introduced in 1969, the overhead-cam four carried a five-speed transmission, electric starter, and an attractive price. While Honda had suspended its racing program in 1967, its competition experience transposed quickly to street machines that were fast, reliable, and relatively simple to maintain.

Taglioni admitted the Japanese talent for effective engineering and manufacturing quality, but had no interest in four-cylinder engines or in building millions of motorcycles. He did want to make high-performance twins in the traditional sport riding framework, and to prove them once again by winning races.

The 750 GT had gained Bologna renewed attention in the States, and the arrival of the 750 Sport raised the Italian flag higher. The bright yellow-orange roadster became the minimalist sport-rodders' bike of the year, and titillated those eagerly awaiting the arrival of the desmo version.
Guy Webster

Racing into History

If the Honda CB 750 signaled the arrival of what would come to be called the Superbike era, the Ducati 750 certified it. Engineer Taglioni had racing in mind from the first, and he and Franco Farne had assembled several 750-cc racing twins in 1971.

The bikes, tested by Bruno Spaggiari and Mike Hailwood, were enlarged versions of the 500-cc GP machine and led directly to the creation of the 750 SS.

Taglioni had been to Daytona a month earlier to have a look at the AMA Formula 750 machines, to get a sense of the competition. He was impressed with the top speeds of the new Kawasaki and Suzuki 750s, which could run 170 miles per hour. But their handling was another matter, and the two-strokes devoured tires at alarming rates. The BSA triples, developed by England's Doug Hele, were also quite rapid but suffered niggling reliability problems. For Taglioni the solution lay in a balanced machine that sacrificed some top speed for enhanced capabilities in handling and longevity.

The Italian 200-miler in April would pit the new racer against Giacomo Agostini's MV Agusta, Walter Villa on Triumph, and a host of Japanese machines assembled for the inaugural "Daytona of Europe" at Imola in 1972.

Promoter Francesco Costa had reportedly mortgaged most of his personal belongings to finance the 200 Miles of Imola, certain that he had a ground floor opportunity to capitalize on the new roadracing format. Ducati technicians, just 25 miles up the road from Imola, hurried to prepare the prototype 750 SS for its public racing debut. The two leading lights on the Ducati team were Bruno Spaggiari, the 39-year-old veteran who had ridden for Ducati since the 1950s, and British star Paul Smart.

"Smartie," who had been riding factory Kawasakis in the U.S. series, had not been Bologna's first choice. Renzo Pasolini, Jarno Saarinen, and Barry Sheene had declined offers, either because of contractual obligations or the not unreasonable notion that a new Ducati twin could not bloody well likely win a 200-mile race. So the call went to Paul, who wasn't even home at the time. When his wife, Maggie, heard the amount of money offered for Smart's appearance, she accepted the ride on his behalf. Smart woman, indeed.

Phil Schilling, then associate editor at *Cycle* magazine, traveled to Bologna the week before the Imola event. He was surprised to find the racing bikes looking quite like production models, which, but for a few bits and pieces, they were. The frames were stock, but fitted with a steering damper and racing shocks, and the front wheel had twin disc brakes with a single disc at the rear. The engines were fitted with new 40-mm Dell'Orto "pumper" carburetors and a high exhaust pipe on the left side. But the most important pieces were the heads and desmodromic valvetrains. Taglioni had transferred the single-cam desmo system from the single intact; with the valve angle at 80 degrees and 10:1 compression, the V-twin made 84 rear-wheel horsepower at 8,800 rpm, and the engine would spin safely to 9,500.

"It was terrific being there just before the race," says Schilling. "Imola was really a big deal. The very notion that it would be called the Daytona of Europe tells you the importance Europeans had attached to American roadracing. This was quite different than it had been just five years earlier, when U.S. racing was considered something of a backwater."

Eight machines were prepared for the Imola 200. The Imola engines were not just 750 GT motors with desmo heads. The three-ring slipper pistons were carried on lightened rods machined from billet, and the alternator was gone from the right side of the crank. The racer used a battery and four coils for ignition in a total-loss twin-plug system; the clutch basket was lightened and the kickstart shaft removed. A hydraulic steering damper was added, and the fork legs were turned down to save weight. Race-ready the bikes weighed 425

Only a few hundred 750 Sports came to the United States; some riders took the option of making the GT a sportier mount. Larry Kahn's 750 GT has adopted another front brake, a Tunstall aftermarket plastic tank, and a Norton-type solo racing saddle. This California metro-retro is still on the road. **Bill McMillan**

This cross-country cafe-racer was a marriage of convenience and necessity. The author bought the Ducati on a visit to Ohio, and was therefore forced by circumstance to ride it home to California. An extra seat pad and the duffle bag were the only concessions to comfort and reality. **John Huetter**

pounds, by racing standards no lightweights.

Schilling attended the pre-race testing session at Modena, the first time the motorcycles would be run at their limits. Spaggiari was up to speed quickly, circulating the rippled airport circuit with consistently quick velocities. Smart added an external steering damper and switched from the Dunlop TT100 to a racing tire on the rear, which settled the Ducati through the rougher portions of the track. Both the engine performance and handling had proven out, and the riders, engineers, and mechanics came away with positive feelings. At the day's end, as Schilling reported, Smart remarked, "You know, this might all work out very well."

Considerable hype preceded the Imola race, which effectively signaled the debut of international superbike racing. MV had agreed to the participation of Giacomo Agostini, 500-cc Grand Prix champion for the past six years running. Ago would ride a special version of the production shaft-drive MV 750 four, fitted with frame, suspension, and brakes from his GP bike. Upcoming GP contender and future world champion Walter Villa was aboard a special Triumph triple prepared by the Italian

This 750 Sport is an all-rounder with a Suzuki bench seat and British cowboy handlebar. Religiously incorrect perhaps, but the bike is certainly handsome in new black-and-gold livery. Tod Rafferty

Bruno Spaggiari, 39, had logged Montjuic victories on Ducati singles in 1957 and 1964. The Italian veteran, with traditional riding style and pudding bowl helmet, was second at Imola. The slot in the front of the fairing directed air to the oil cooler mounted on the steering head.

importer, and Moto Guzzi entered a tricked-up V7 Sport. The field was filled with machines from BSA, Laverda, Honda, Suzuki, and Kawasaki. More than 70,000 spectators crowded the 3.19 circuit on the day of the race.

The race unfolded as if the script had been written in Bologna. Paul Smart and Bruno Spaggiari finished 1 and 2 with an average speed of 98 miles per hour and shared with Agostini the fastest lap honors at 100 miles per hour. The home crowd was ecstatic over Ducati's stunning victory, the paddock bubbled with champagne and Italian euphoria, and factory officials promised that yes, Imola replicas would soon be available to the riding public. But *domani* in Italian, much like *mañana* in Spanish, doesn't necessarily mean tomorrow, or even the day after. It just means not today . . . we're working on it . . . we'll let you know. Not to worry.

In 1973, Ducati returned to the scene of its stunning victory with a significantly revised 750. Included valve angle was narrowed from 80 to 60 degrees, while more bore (86 mm) and less stroke (64.5 mm) promised higher performance through a loftier redline. The wheelbase was shortened, three rear axle positions added more adjustability, and new chain-adjuster eccentrics were incorporated at the swingarm pivot.

Although the new model was lighter and faster, the handling had lost considerable high-speed precision in the process. But the chassis responded to a simple fix: fitting the triple clamps from the leading-axle fork to the center-axle tubes bumped the trail considerably, and the handling improved (although steering was slowed). This was another hurry-up project, delayed by a metal workers' strike, and the racer was barely ready for Imola. Nonetheless, Spaggiari came second to Jarno Saarinen's Yamaha in the race.

Taglioni now shifted his focus to the production models, fashioned in the configuration he had originally conceived. The production version of the Imola racers would not appear until 1974, but in the meantime Ducati issued the 750 Sport, which boasted an uprated engine with higher compression and open 32-mm Dell'Ortos replacing the GT's filtered 30-mm Amals.

With a 9.5:1 compression, the Sport made about 60 horsepower, good for 130 miles per hour. With genuine clip-on handlebars, rearset footpegs, *monoposto* (single seat), and sexier styling, the 750 S offered a marvelously sporting alternative to the GT but fell far short of an "Imola replica."

The first Stateside report on the 750 Sport appeared in the January 1973 issue of *Cycle* magazine (see sidebar). The editors noted the Spartan riding position and heavy low-speed handling, but wrote that the Sport was built "for honking hard along back roads. At this task the machine is simply superb." The test bike had just come from winning a five-hour production race at Mosport, Canada.

Horsepower of the Press

The *Cycle* staffers, a mixed bag of gearheads, journalists, racers, and technoids, embraced the Ducati 750 twins shamelessly. They made no bones about their lust for the machines, but took some pains to itemize all the deficiencies a prospective owner was likely to encounter. This was perceived in some quarters as either a high standard of journalistic integrity at work, or a shameless bit of pettifogging designed to ensure a steady supply of the motorcycles for themselves. Perhaps it was a bit of both, but the magazine would, until the end of its run in 1991, remain a Ducati-friendly forum.

Nearly everyone who rode the first 750 Sports bought one, and the model did not come to the United States in great numbers. Total production for two years was about 2,000, and the majority were sold in Italy,

Smart was among the first roadracers to hang off the motorcycle in turns to provide an added measure of ground clearance. The style quickly gained adherents around the world. The Dunlop stickers, absent during the race, were apparently added later for publicity photos.

England, and Australia. Unofficial figures put the number of Sports exported to the United States at around 250. Some riders, including those few with inside information, decided to save their money for the Super Sport, which was to be along soon. *Domani.*

Despite its less sporting pretensions, however, the GT continued to accumulate praise, and fans. Gordon Jennings recalls his own Ducati 750 GT. "It was a terrific motorcycle. They had a road test bike at *Cycle* magazine and everybody just fell in love with the damn thing. It was absolutely marvelous; they were very steady, handling was a little heavy, but the things were extraordinarily steady. And we had all those backroads to entertain ourselves on, and did. I think Dale Boller and Cook Neilson both bought them. Anyway, they bought me one! As kind of a present for being old and disagreeable.

"At *Cycle* one time, a guy was there from Harley-Davidson, and I had just ridden into the shop on mine. Cook and everybody were telling him how terrific the Ducati was compared with the Harley. And Jess Thomas said `watch this,' and he reached over and started the thing with his hand; just grabbed the kickstart lever and pushed. The Harley guy was dumbstruck."

Hard on the heels of the GT, the Ducati 750 Sport proved the Euro-style cafe racer's commercial viability in the States, even though the market segment was still a distinct minority. Taglioni wasn't seriously concerned with the numbers; the design had been confirmed at Imola, the performance reviews in the enthusiast press were positive, and the real Imola replica, the 750 SS, was in the wings. Life was good in Bologna, and although the Italian government/labor/management equation was always subject to sudden revision for reasons not always apparent, Dr. T. carried on designing the motorcycles he wanted to see built. The first run of Super Sports in 1973 were Sports with desmo heads; the engine covers were painted black and Veglia instruments sat atop the center-axle Marzocchi fork. Unlike the leading-axle fork on the Sport, the SS sliders carried the brake calipers in front.

In 1970, Cook Neilson had succeeded Gordon Jennings as editor of *Cycle* magazine. A drag racing enthusiast, Neilson had built and successfully campaigned several Harley-powered slingshots in the East, but when the Ziff-Davis Publishing Company relocated the magazine from New York to California in 1972, he found only limited drag-racing activity. He also discovered plenty of twisty roads, sunshine, and the new Ducati V-twins,

Cycle Magazine

Cycle magazine was founded in 1950 by Bob Petersen of Petersen Publishing, as a companion to his popular *Hot Rod* magazine. After losing interest in the two-wheeled market, Petersen (who later acquired *Motorcyclist*) sold his original title to Floyd Clymer, motorcycle racer, dealer, entrepreneur, evangelist, publisher, and inventor of the Clymer Through-the-Windshield spotlight for automobiles. When U.S. motorcycling came of age in the 1960s, the journals serving the sport advanced in kind. Ziff-Davis Publishing bought the *Cycle* imprint in 1966 and moved the office from California to New York, where its *Car and Driver* magazine was headquartered. Gordon Jennings, then technical editor at *Cycle World*, was persuaded to take the helm, and Cook Neilson was hired as an associate editor, followed by Phil Schilling.

This group formed the nucleus that moved American motorcycle journalism from a largely hobbyist enterprise into the professional arena. Returned to California in 1972, the magazine had improved steadily and continued elevating the standards for reporting, feature writing, technical information, and race coverage. *Cycle* was sold to CBS in 1985, which also published *Cycle World*. Both magazines went through several more corporate swaps and were eventually acquired by Hachette-Filipacchi. Faced with what seemed to be a dwindling market, Hachette discontinued *Cycle* in 1991.

The works of two *Cycle* pioneers still appear in contemporary monthlies—Gordon Jennings in *Motorcyclist* and Kevin Cameron in *Cycle World*.

however, and that Southern California was home to a legion of talented riders, tuners, and specialized motocraftsfolk. Aided and abetted by Phil Schilling, and Jennings, who had returned to California earlier, Neilson perceived the opportunity to become a roadracer. His five-year quest would be chronicled in *Cycle* with a series of articles titled "Beyond Racer Road."

After Imola, the single greatest promotional boost for Ducati in the 1970s issued from Westlake Village, California. *Cycle* staffers were buying the V-twins as quickly as they arrived at ZDS Motors, the western distributor in Los Angeles, and in little more than a year had snapped up nine Ducatis of their own. While this effective endorsement did no harm to the sales of the Bologna twins, the reviewers' praise of the engine and chassis were always accompanied by an itemized list of the motorcycle's faults.

On the Super Sport: "Stress cracks spread from every attachment point of fiberglass to chassis. The bottom of the fuel tank leaks in two places. The front fender cannot be made to fit properly. The seat is tatty. The tachometer, pirated from the Sport, has the red line set at 7800 rpm when it ought to be at 9000. The fairing

The Imola effect served Ducati well for years. Clinton Kendall's 1974 "Imola GT" has a chrome-moly steel replica of the 1973 frame with the engine raised 1 inch. A Dyna S ignition, hydraulic clutch, and Gailbreath pipes complete the package. The inset shows the pickup for the Avocet electronic tach. Clinton Kendall

Given the Imola victory, the 750 Super Sport was an icon before it even went into production. Published figures on the number of original 1974 Super Sports built have varied with time, from 200 to 400 to 450. Few, in any case, which has ensured their status as prized collectibles. Guy Webster

fits asymmetrically. Rust is intruding through the surface of the frame's rather shoddy paint (that doesn't match the rather shoddy paint on the tank, seat or fender). The fuse box is mounted upside-down and is open to the punishment of lousy weather. A hole has been crudely filed in the rear inner-fender to make room for the rear brake line. And there's an honest-to-God Italian fly, molded into the fiberglass fuel tank."

And the first test of the 750 Sport concluded ". . . the Ducati 750, in any of its three incarnations, is still the best handling street machine available. The 750 Sport has a great engine packaged with a brilliant chassis. Period. But be warned. You'd better love that engine, and love that running gear. If you don't, sure as hell you're going to be disappointed with the motorcycle."

Editor Neilson soon availed himself of the opportunity to ride Southern California's racer roads with more experienced corner carvers on the magazine staff, and proved a quick study. "Finally it got to where it no longer made any kind of sense to ride at that pace in two-way traffic," he says. So his initial Ducati 750 GT soon made the transition from road to track.

Riverside Raceway immediately revealed the limitations of both bike and rider, and the first adjustments were to increase both the engine's compression (with Sport pistons) and the size of the rear tire. The next upgrade included heads ported by flow-bench guru Jerry Branch, who also installed Harley XR intake valves, S&W valve springs, and a Norris high-lift/duration camshaft. Gordon Jennings fiddled the throats of the Amal carburetors and the Ducati was ready for the AMA's inaugural production race at Laguna Seca.

Armed with new zeal and energy in early practice, Neilson suddenly found himself corkscrewed into the macadam and left with a bashed, bent, and punctured Ducati and a broken finger. Quick patchwork put bike and rider back on the track, and Neilson managed a sixth-place finish in the race and was lapped only by Yvon duHamel, who "could ride a lambchop past a wolf," said Neilson.

The quest for more power led to even hotter cams made by Sig Erson and swapping the Amals for Dell'Orto carburetors; Dunlop racing tires replaced the K81s and a second disc brake was fitted to the front. Neilson and Schilling arrived at Ontario Raceway with a new weapon, which proved faster than class-of-the-class Reg Pridmore's blistering Butler & Smith BMW. But catching Reg and passing him proved two different propositions, and Neilson admitted he still had much to learn of the roadracer's craft. Then, absent Pridmore but against worthy competitors, Neilson won the next three races and decided that production roadracing was neat stuff. The 750 GT was returned to street trim and plans laid for lashing up a more serious mount for the next season, the Ducati 750 SS that would come to be known as the *California Hot Rod*.

The bike's desmo valve gear promised higher revs and more agressive valve timing, just as it did in the late 1950s. Gordon Jennings, back on the staff at *Cycle* as the technical editor reported: "With the desmo, mainly you get away from the problem of valve-spring surge. You can accelerate the valve really hard on opening, instead of being limited by the characteristics of valve springs, as long as you keep it at a load level that doesn't break through the oil film separating the cam and the follower. Below that, everything goes; so you can really punch 'em open fast and yank 'em closed the same way, and it works real well. Racing engines wear out valve springs in a horrendous hurry."

Tweaking the Twins

By mid-1973 the Ducati product planners had decided that a larger engine was needed, in response to the prodigious ponies of the 903-cc Kawasaki Z-1. An 864-cc version of the 750 SS, ridden by Benjamin Grau and Salvador Canellas, had just won the demanding 24 Hours of Montjuich in Barcelona, reinforcing the Imola imagery and generating more publicity. While still committed to racing by independent satellite teams, Ducati management was more eager to contend with the increasingly

popular Japanese touring models, and pressed the need for a more competitive motorcycle in the general market.

The result in 1975 was the 860 GT, descended from the original 750, but with a number of changes to the engine and bodywork. The valvetrain employed conventional springs, and straight-cut gears carried power to the cam drives, which now featured outboard bearing supports. The breaker points were gone in favor of electronic ignition, and an oil filter was situated in the former ignition housing. Milder cams were used in the 860 and valve adjustment changed to the screw and locknut system. The new engine side-cases were sculpted in the angular block fashion of the bodywork, which prompted their informal "square-case" designation.

The styling of the 860 GT was the work of Giorgetto Giugiaro of Italdesign. Although acknowledged as a prominent automotive stylist whose work ranged from the Maserati Ghibli to the Volkswagen Scirocco, his angular motif transposed less gracefully to motorcycles. The Ducati twin had little common aesthetic ground with any four-wheeler, and seemed to resist Giugiaro's planar surfaces. What had been a dynamic form was rendered static. Some enthusiasts thought it looked rather like a wheeled suitcase, or a motorcycle still half in the crate. And the seamed Lafranconi mufflers didn't help. Despite the almost unanimously negative reception in the market, the same styling was applied the following year to the star-crossed GTL 350 and 500, parallel twins.

By the mid-1970s the Honda CB 350 and 450 twins had sold in record numbers in the United States, and Ducati felt obliged to offer middleweight machines in the same price and performance category. Sales of

The Grand Touring configuration of a modified 1974 GT: hydraulic clutch, homemade rearsets, double discs, BuB mufflers, and Krauser luggage, in doeskin tan and Indian metallic brown. Clinton Kendall

DUCATI 860

The Stateside reception for the 860GT barely rose to lukewarm. The female models in the earlier round-case ads wore less clothing, as did the motorcycles. And both, truth be told, looked better. The Ducati's Giugiaro bodywork did go with the high-heeled boots and designer jeans.

the singles were dwindling, and Bologna had nothing to offer the mass of riders either unable to afford, or intimidated by, the big V-twins.

Unfortunately the design of the GTL series rendered their other qualities moot. The massive crankcases seemed odd on engines of medium displacement, and the performance did nothing to offset the appearance. Economy of manufacture dictated the use of a chain-driven overhead cam, but the twin's 180-degree crankshaft imposed a vibration penalty at lower rpm. The twin did maintain the Ducati tradition for precise handling, but the curb weight of 430 pounds, and a price over $1,800, put the GTL 500 at a serious disadvantage.

Just as they had done with the Monza Junior ten years earlier, the design deciders at Ducati had switched from round to square shapes, and this time their influence had spread beyond the bodywork to the engine. Some observers began to wonder if Ducati may not have fallen under an ancient Roman curse, enforcing a return to some notion of architectural simplicity. Or perhaps the durability of Italian designer genes had finally played itself out over the millennia. It was even suggested that an ancient, pagan form of mythical Gaulish retribution obliged Italian craftsmen to shoot themselves in the foot at least once each decade, just to get their own attention.

So Ducati had to face the self-imposed problem created by building real motorcycles under fictitious bodywork. And given their considerable investment in both the 860 GT and the parallel twins, the company needed to move quickly if it was to salvage any sort of return on the new models. Not *domani*.

First in line for the fix was the 860, now designated

After Imola, Bruno Spaggiari formed his own team. The second run of 750 Super Sports had the center-axle fork, Scarab brakes, 230-mm discs, and nondragging right-side exhaust pipe. The Scuderia Spaggiari Ducati was dominant in the hands of young Franco Uncini, who would later become 500 GP champion. Tod Rafferty

the GTS, with more traditional shapes for the seat and fuel tank, an improved electric starter, Smiths instruments, and twin disc front brakes. By consensus it was a more attractive machine than the GT, and still well in possession of the traditional Ducati traits for power delivery, handling, and transubstantiation of inspirational confidence at speed. But it was still cobby. The troublesome electronic ignition of the GT had been supplanted by a new unit with a transistorized voltage regulator, and compression got bumped to 9.8:1. The subframe was revised to lower the seat height, but the machine still didn't look right to the Ducatisti, and the seat was still too hard. And the engine seeped oil from several joints.

Some would argue that attempts to civilize the Ducati twin were misguided from the outset, since it was, after all, conceived as a sportbike. Others, with perhaps a more substantial purchase on the handlebars of economic reality, would suggest that Bologna's comfort and convenience fitments were simply half-hearted and poorly executed. The 860 then became the 900 GTS, a marketing move that reflected no change in the 864-cc displacement. Improvements were in the works, however, and by 1978 the GT series evolved into the Darmah desmo editions, and begat the Mike Hailwood Replica models, which would mark the end of the bevel-drive cam period of Ducati history.

The GTL 350- and 500-cc parallel twins would have a shorter lifespan. Taglioni had little to do with these engines, given his unsatisfactory experience with the similar prototypes built in the 1960s. Ducati had

enlisted Italjet's Leo Tartarini to restyle both the 860 and the parallel twin, with assembly of the latter now handled mostly in his factory. The second iteration of the 500 saw the adoption of the desmo valve gear and a double downtube frame, but while the appearance generated more positive comments the performance showed no corresponding improvement. The engine still produced annoying midrange vibration and made little power below 7,000 rpm. And the 500 Desmo Sport was

still more expensive. The final versions were the non-desmo 350 and 500 GTV that appeared in 1978 and remained in production into 1983. Only a few of the parallel twins were exported, and the models were soon superseded by the V-twin Pantah.

But powerful and increasingly sophisticated four-cylinder Japanese motorcycles now dominated the U.S. market by huge margins. Plus, Honda, Yamaha, Suzuki, and Kawasaki had not only rewritten the rules worldwide for sport and touring motorcycles, now they began producing single-cylinder dual-purpose bikes, serving the same motorcycling segment that Ducati had only recently abandoned. That's how they get you, mumbled the Italians (and, rather later, their Milwaukee counterparts), by building our stuff and making it better. Those rascals. Thus the catalyst provided by Soichiro Honda pulled Ducati, and the other few remaining non-Japanese motorcycle companies, their long second steps into the 20th century.

The Japanese success had, of course, provoked many of the miss-steps made by other companies that

were scrambling in the catch-up mode. But it also worked to elevate the manufacturing quality, assembly, and subsequent reliability of all motorcycles; the Japanese motorcycle phenomenon even affected perceptions of engineering and design within other motorcycle companies, if only by default. Ducati took the lesson that building its own version of a Japanese motorcycle was a blind alley. American car manufacturers were now being invited by their stockholders to attend the same seminars. In the mid-1970s the Japanese, who had overwhelmed motorcycling worldwide in ten years, decided to take it up a notch.

Those who managed to follow suit then or later (Ducati, Harley-Davidson, Cagiva, and BMW) came to build far better motorcycles. Those who for various reasons could not (Triumph, BSA, Norton, Benelli, Gilera, Laverda, MV Agusta, and almost Moto Guzzi) drifted into history. But if what goes around does indeed come around, and so it would appear, several of these marques have returned. Nearly all are quite different from their ancestors in both design and execution, more Japanese in terms of build-quality and detailing, and all under new ownership. But returned nonetheless, which has become cause for attaboys among the enthusiasts of motorcycle diversity and multiple choice.

Old Blue the Overdog

By 1975 the Neilson/Schilling 750 SS was up to speed, and the velocity (142 miles per hour) had many of their competitors convinced that the engine must have gained some displacement. Now dubbed Old Blue, but still a 750, the desmo twin racked up eight class wins and four overall victories in ten races; a flat tire and clogged fuel tank vent caused two DNFs respectively. At Daytona the *Cycle* twin was top 750 and fifth overall. For 1976 the AMA deleted the 750 class and Superbike Production became a 1,000-cc formula, stipulating stock frames and lighting, standard carburetors, and original muffler shells. The rule change pushed the Overdog into its ultimate phase of both horsepower and handling.

First the heads went once again to Jerry Branch's flow bench, and the crankcases and cylinders were off to be bored to accept Ducati 450 liners. The factory deluxe crankshafts, 900 SS cylinders and pistons, carbs, manifolds, and such were ordered from Bologna, but three months passed with no parts delivered. Neilson and Schilling couldn't wait for the day after *domani*.

With less than two months before Daytona, the California Hot Rod quickly evolved as a wonder of West Coast ingenuity and local technology. The engine, now at 883 cc, had Venolia pistions, Yamaha 500 rings, and Toyota wrist pins. Master fabricator Pierre desRoches had reinforced the frame, and made up titanium axles and a magnesium rear caliper carrier. The bike ran 145 miles per hour at Daytona, where Neilson finished third behind the Butler & Smith BMWs of Steve McLaughlin and Reg Pridmore. Neilson admitted he was down on experience in terms of dealing with traffic, braking, and the severe demands on rider concentration imposed by long races.

His abilities, and the Overdog's bits and pieces, both moving and non-moving parts, were subjected to a steady curriculum of refinement for the rest of the 1976 season. With more trick parts machined by desRoches, the Ducati began a weight-loss program

that brought it down to under 400 pounds ready to race. "The gearbox was a real pain in the butt," Neilson recalls. "The teeth would bend under load, then the case-hardening would begin to pit. We never lost a gear tooth, thanks to Bob Gorsuch, who would pick up impending failure under Magnafluxing. The guy who made the difference was Marvin Webster from Mill Valley. Tim Witham, the W in S&W shocks, told him we were worth helping. Web, who used to make transmissions for Indy cars, made two gearsets for us in special vacuum-remelt steel that he got out the back door of a Sikorsky helicopter plant in Texas."

By 1977 the racer had lost the tail-mounted oil cooler, now deemed unnecessary. It was replaced by a Volkswagen oil filter, mounted just behind the steering head, which fed oil to the left-side cam bearings. Gordon Jennings had done an article on motorcycle ignition coils, and found that the best performance came from

The iconic status of the 750 Super Sports restricts them largely to private collections, museums, and a few living rooms—few turn up regularly at vintage racing events. Italy's Del Biondo Racing offers a large menu of performance parts for bevel-drive singles and twins. Tod Rafferty

Cook Neilson is ready for the finals at Daytona. Phil Schilling answers the "how did you make it go so fast" question. He credits Taglioni, Ducati, Jerry Branch, Pierre desRoches, Neilson, trial-and-error development, patience, determination, and the magic of Kmart coils. Tom Riles

Kmart coils that sold for about $6 a piece. Adding the discount coils, a ballast resistor, and welding up the centrifugal advance mechanism gave Old Blue a strong and reliable spark.

"Cook really started to get serious about racing with the 750 SS," recalls Jennings, "and he kept running into problems. The very first was that they were delivered stock with closing springs, just to make sure the valves closed at low speeds and for starting it. As it happened I had some earlier history with desmo engines, second-hand, but I still knew about it. Mercedes-Benz, when they built the M196 engines, had closing springs and the first time they ran the engine on the dyno, all the

closing springs shattered. They made a couple more tries, and then decided to just leave the springs out and see what happened. Well, the engine started and ran perfectly without those stupid springs in there. Even at low speed; when that intake valve would get near the seat . . . there may have been a slight amount of back-flow, but rising pressure in the cylinder would just slam it shut and that was it.

"Then Lance Reventlow's ill-fated Scarab GT car had a four-cylinder engine designed by old Leo Goosen, which had desmo valve action. And it had closing springs. And the first time they started it up, the closing springs broke. So Cook got his desmo, and the closing springs broke. And

Cook: We all set? Phil: I think so. I've got your sunglasses, the other spark plugs, and the towel. Not real sure we've got enough duct tape on these number plates, though. How much time have we got? Never mind. Did you put gas in it? I think I'm going to throw up.

I told him about these instances, and that the springs were superfluous. So he left the springs out and it ran fine.

"One of the big improvements in that engine, that went with the bigger bore, was a completely different piston/head configuration. I'd had a really illuminating conversation once with Doug Hele, who did the all-conquering Triumphs at Daytona. He was a brilliant engine-development guy, and he said you need to make a piston crown like you were filling the combustion chamber from bottom to top with water. Just fit everything really tightly except where you need valve cutouts, and a flat top on the dome. So I told Cook that, and he went at it in a pretty clever way. He took a cylinder and head, put some parting agent around the bore in the combustion chamber and poured

epoxy in it. When it had set up he had himself a perfect fit, and machined the valve pockets in that big lump, and stuck the thing in place and poured oil in the plug hole to see what kind of compression ratio he had. On the first try it was somewhere near diesel, and I guesstimated that about 10.5 would be good. So he would take the slug out and machine more flat off the top and stick it back in. As I recall, he stopped cutting at 10.8, and then took the polyester slug off to the people who were making the pistons and said make the dome like that. And they did."

Phil Schilling now maintains a U.S. registry of Ducati 750 SS owners, which numbers about 60. "Yes, I remember that we threw the closing springs out. Also, Neilson was a voracious researcher. If Cook thought the president of the United States might be a useful source of Ducati information, he would have called the White House and gotten the president on the line. And Pierre desRoches was very good with frame and suspension jobs, and he got that way by trying to stabilize the frames on Kawasaki Z-1s. He was sort of a natural, seat-of-the-pants engineer, although he didn't have an engineering degree. And he was a very accomplished fabricator; some of the stuff we copied from factory bikes, but Pierre added to that. He was also good with suspension, and spent a lot of time getting a front fork to work really well. He was also fun to work with, always upbeat.

"One of the great secrets of the California Hot Rod was slick tires. That bike could fully exploit slicks in a

Probably one of the few people not surprised that Neilson had won at Daytona was Neilson. He knew the Ducati held a demonstrable edge in handling through the infield, and that an early lead could carry the race. If it didn't break, and he made no mistakes, he could win. And so it was. Tom Riles

The Darmah took its name from the tiger in a popular Italian children's adventure series. The Ducati version was more of a pussycat, with a modified 860 frame and electric starter. The desmo heads were fed by 32-mm carburetors and spark was delivered by a Bosch electronic ignition. Guy Webster

way that other bikes couldn't. That sucker really worked, and Neilson said on more than one occasion that he was the only guy who really knew how good that bike was. Because he was riding it, and it could do things that other bikes just couldn't do, mostly just stick like glue around corners. And it was a good bike to learn on, because the Ducatis tended to do things slowly; there were no nasty little quirks that popped up in a nanosecond and had you off.

"Cook knew the bike was better than he was at first," Schilling says. "But in very short order, and especially by the time we got to Daytona in 1977, my feeling was that he was absolutely as good as the bike. He was a very accomplished rider. And the harder he worked at it, the more gifted he became. He thought about it a lot, took a very cerebral approach to racing. And it was a pleasure to work with him; it was fun."

The team had ended the 1976 season on a disappointing note, with a DNF caused by the gearshift mechanism at Laguna Seca. They took encouragement, however, from a practice session held at the track a week earlier, when Kenny Roberts was in attendance for a press conference. Roberts asked for a ride on the Ducati, which was immediately granted, including the use of Neilson's leathers and Steve Baker's helmet. Roberts took to the track as Phil and Cook waited, "anxious as old maids" to hear the national champion's impressions.

"It's really nice," Roberts said when he pulled in. "The back brake doesn't work at all. The front end's too

stiff, and it has too much geometry. The back end's too stiff, too, and you're using too much tire back there. But the motor's really nice. I didn't have any idea these production bikes made that much power. Hey, it's fast. Bet I could run 1:14s on this track with it." (Laguna Seca was then a shorter and faster circuit.) The editor-racers were pleased that an accomplished Yamaha TZ750 pilot was impressed with the Ducati's engine.

Ducati enthusiasts in the United States and Europe had followed the serial adventures of the *Cycle* project racer for more than three years. It was almost like waiting for the next installment of *Mighty Mouse* at the Bijou. At Daytona in 1977 Old Blue was gridded against the San Jose BMW entry with David Emde aboard, Mike Baldwin on a Reno Leoni Moto Guzzi, and Wes Cooley riding a Yoshimura Kawasaki Z-1. Real racers, one and all, and each fielding a potent weapon. Neilson's strategy was to avoid a direct scuffle with Cooley or Emde, and utilize the Ducati's handling advantage in the infield without being vacuumed up by the horsepower kings on the straights.

"I therefore wanted to clear out as quickly as I could and jam the Duck around the track at full honk for at least 10 laps before even looking back. On the 9th of 14 laps I felt my left knee touch the pavement in turn one. Since that rarely happens I figured the time had come to check out what was going on behind, and ease up if further berserko riding was not called for."

It was not. His competitors were not in sight. Cooley had run second on the Kawasaki until his brakes went south and he was overtaken by Dave Emde on the BMW. The magazine racers had done it—after three years of research, trial and error, crashes, and creative tweaking and tuning, victory was theirs. Doubly gratifying was the subsequent engine teardown back in California, which revealed little or no wear on the major components.

"There was only one cam profile available," recalls Neilson, "the Imola, so we didn't have to spend a lot of time and money dithering around in an area that is mind-numbing in its complexity. We had absolutely no problems with the cylinder heads, and since these heads were unique in the world, that was a godsend. And all that desmo stuff was fascinating to Phil and me—beautiful, intricate, fun to work on. To hold a complete and perfectly-adjusted cylinder head in your hands, rotate the tower shaft and see and feel the valves opening and closing with just exactly the right amount of resistance was for me almost a religious experience. I loved setting up the cylinder heads. So did Phil."

Boxing the Bevelers

Ducati proudly advertised the Daytona win in Europe, but had no immediate supply of corresponding product to fill the ensuing demand. The 750 SS was already headed for history, to be displaced by less expensive machines with wider market appeal. From the Imola victory in 1972 to Old Blue at Daytona in 1977, the Ducati logo had remained at the forefront of high-performance motorcycling around the globe. But the factory remained unable to transfer the success to the general marketplace in any profitable numbers.

While the racing victories had been great for the company's sporting image, the heroics went unreflected by the balance sheet. Ducati had, in fact, been steadily losing larger sums of money throughout the mid-1970s, and the company was on the market. The government finance corporation controlling Ducati was eager to see

some profits, the absence of which would find the company reconfigured to manufacture something other than motorcycles. Taglioni then had two protoypes on the road, a 350-cc single and 500-cc twin, both of which featured belt-drive single overhead-cam heads. Lack of financing killed the single and the twin would come to market as the Pantah. But the 900 SS, recently transmogrified from the 860 GTS, helped maintain market interest among sporting enthusiasts.

However, profitability notwithstanding, the Ducati 750 twins were the last of the traditional Anglo-European roadburners. The gear lever was on the right side, in natural balance with the left-hand clutch; likewise the left-foot rear and right-hand front brakes. The machines were handcrafted for spirited application in the classic continental style of motoring smartly down the road, civilians and the constabulary be damned. The properly

The square-case 900 SS arrived in 1975, the first and most favored of the model's seven-year series. The first run, about 250 each of 750s and 900s, still had the right-side gearshift. These were 860 engines with desmo heads and Conti mufflers, Brembo brakes, and an Imola-style fuel tank.
Guy Webster

Purveyors of aftermarket bodywork, engine parts, and accessories have helped maintain the supply of bevelers still in service. The brotherhood of bevelheads has no national organization or regular meetings, but they do ride their motorcycles. Bill McMillan

adjusted Ducati (or Moto Guzzi, Laverda, BMW, Norton, BSA, or Triumph) would run at the limits of visibility, traction, and rider ability for hours without complaint, or at least until it was time to stop for coffee. The cafe racer was built to ride, and was not useful for sightseeing, touring, or trips to the market, or for transporting passengers, luggage, or camping supplies.

Another element of this historical juncture was the shift in riding styles. No better contrast exists than the distinctions between Bruno Spaggiari and Paul Smart at Imola in 1972. Spaggiari, the 39-year-old veteran, rode in the classic manner with his back straight, head upright, and butt centered on the machine. Paul Smart applied the emerging low-crouch, hanging-off, knee-out style, a posture also employed by the great Jarno Saarinen. A few years later Kenny Roberts would institute

knee-dragging as requisite roadracing form.

As motorcycles grew larger and wider they had developed a corresponding decrease in ground clearance, and cornering without dragging hardware required climbing off to the inside and holding up the machine. Many of these motorcycles also wobbled fiercely, tending to distract the rider only half on the seat and turn him into a lever. But the Ducati 750, by virtue of its balance, stability, and neutral demeanor, did not impose any particular style on the rider.

The performance parameters were defined only by its steering acuity, ground clearance, and coefficient of tractive power transfer. The rider could be playing Scrabble, so long as the motorcycle was properly pointed, leaned, and throttled. The Ducati engine, chassis, and running gear transmitted a reassuring sense of calm at the eye of the storm; do nothing extraordinarily stupid, it said, and you will be delivered home safe and sound. And probably in first place.

The next step in Ducati's marketing and design shift to the all-purpose roadster was the 900 GTS. The Aprilia switchgear was replaced by more functional and reliable CEV units, and stainless-steel fenders supplanted the earlier painted guards. But the Giugiaro styling stayed out of favor, and the GTS was soon further distilled into the Darmah SD, named after the tiger in a popular Italian folk tale. The Tartarini styling, with a swoopy tail section and generic fuel tank accented with a racing stripe, met with wider approval. The "civilized" desmo, as several publications characterized it, the Darmah achieved more mainstream response and allowed the more heretical 900 SS to remain the gentleman's express for solo sorties on the back roads.

Although derived from what many considered the most pedestrian of Ducati V-twins, the Darmah successfully introduced what would come to be called the sport-touring motorcycle. Creature comforts were addressed with a better electric starter, Nippondenso switchgear, more powerful alternator, Bosch electronic ignition, and air filters. The revised frame brought the seat height down, and the Campagnolo cast mag wheels added the requisite racy touch. The engine wore 32-mm carburetors but retained the magic of desmodromic valving, and retained the fat and lusty spread of booming urge (although the rolling thunder was severely subdued by the chintzy-looking seamed mufflers).

The Darmah came to represent Bologna's improving grasp of the demographic straddle; or the ability to serve both ends of the "consumer base profile," also called having it both ways, or, in the popular idiom, playing both ends against the middle. In Bologna it finally seemed the only reasonable manner to keep Ducati in business, and not find themselves compelled to design and build widget motors. The Darmah may have come a few years late, but it lasted six years, a time frame that would also account for Ducati's remaining lifespan as a semi-independent company.

Taglioni had not been pleased with the 860 GT, but consented to restyle the engine cases to complement the Giugiaro bodywork. The 750 and 900 Super Sports were both built in 1975 with the square-case engines of the 860; the trick rods of the original 750 SS were replaced, but the desmo valvetrain and 40-mm carburetors remained, and the Conti mufflers. The first square-

Mike Hailwood seemed every bit the racer at 38 that he had been at 18. Perhaps better. Some opined that his encore could only have happened at the Isle of Man, where he was the master. A week later he beat Read again at Mallory Park, a scratcher's circuit.

case desmo also retained the right-side shift lever, no longer approved for the U.S. market. Since fewer than 500 of the models were built, Ducati wasn't concerned with configuring them to American specifications. The Marzocchi fork carried leading-caliper Brembo brakes with radially drilled cast-iron rotors; the rear brake was also a Brembo unit. The second generation Imola replica also kept the Smiths instruments of the originals.

While the new 900 SS remained the handsome prince of cafe racer styling, the boxed engine covers were at odds with the flowing shapes surrounding them. The civilizing process had eliminated the racing-style fuel tank, Campagnola wheels, and right-side shift lever, but the racing kit was still offered with lumpy cams, oil cooler, high pipes, and fairing. Many riders simply replaced the 32-mm carbs and seamed mufflers with 40-mm units and Contis once the bikes had been registered. Although some hard-boiled sport riders initially perceived the 900 SS as merely a Darmah in cafe racer trim, the SS was some 30 pounds lighter. And while performance figures for the two models were roughly equal, with the big carbs and Contis the SS was a half-second quicker and 5 miles an hour faster in the quarter-mile.

While the chassis retained the design integrity of the original 750 SS, the civility program had bestowed improvements on many ancillary bits of the 900 (which remained 864 cc). The electronic ignition proved generally trustworthy, imposed no disadvantage on the engine's performance, and required no constant adjustment. The Brembo brakes worked well, as did the 38-mm Marzocchi fork. Despite the jiggery-pokery employed to fit the shift lever on the left side, the gearchange action was only slighty diminished. In 1978 a new shift mechanism eliminated the right-to-left crossover shaft. The ignition switch moved to the instrument panel, and the electrical control switches worked reliably. Most important, the big end bearings had been improved to solve earlier reliability problems.

But in comparable market terms, the SS was still a limited production motorcycle. As the horsepower wars in Japan continued to escalate, the numbers of 750 Super Sports dwindled as more emphasis was given the 900. In 1978, its final year, only 30 were built, com-

pared to 1,037 of the 900s. In 1979 the Campagnola rims returned on the 900, which was finished in black with gold trim. With the introduction of the Pantah, and the advent of the Mike Hailwood Replica, the 900 SS began to fade away. Minor detail changes were made in the last editions in 1981; the ignition system was improved, and the gearshift mechanism simplified. The dual seat became standard and the solo saddle deleted as an option. In another year the eight-year run of the 900 SS drew to a close, with total production of 6,323 machines. Only 599 of the second-generation 750 SS were built.

The Michael Hailwood Hallelujah

The Italian state regulators were no longer persuaded that a racing department was essential to Ducati's designated profit projection, so the race shop effectively went out the back door, around the corner, and down the street a bit. Nepoti Caracchi Racing (NCR), founded by Giorgio Nepoti and Rino Caracchi, had specialized in Ducati racing specials for five years. In 1973 the shop effectively became Ducati's outside racing department, and worked directly with Franco

The Isle of Man win poster has been reprinted often these past two decades. On some the colors have faded, but the Hailwood legacy is cast in permanent hues among those who saw him ride and those who raced with him, who will forever remember him as the motorcycle roadracer of the century, the "shy superstar."

Isle of Man - 2 June 1978 Driver Mike Hailwood

Farne as liaison with the factory. Projects that could not be developed under the watchful eyes of government auditors were transferred to NCR, which developed special parts and supplied them to Ducati dealers and independent racers. One of their customers was Steve Wynne at Sports Motor Cycles in Manchester, England.

Mike Hailwood had retired from motorcycle racing in 1967. Only 27 at the time, he had won nine world championships and 12 TT titles at the Isle of Man. His first Gran Prix win, the Ulster 125 GP in 1959, was taken aboard a Ducati. Hailwood went on to win the Formula Two car championship in 1972 and had a promising career in Formula One, but in 1974 a crash at the Nurburgring resulted in a badly broken right leg, which left him limited movement of the foot. Hailwood then retired from motor racing and moved with his family to New Zealand, where he went into the marine engine business. Within two years he was bored silly.

Hailwood then rode a few vintage races in Australia, and the old impulse returned and stayed. He hadn't raced motorcycles for 10 years, except for the Daytona 200 in 1970 and 1971, and in both he retired early with a broken BSA triple. (Dick Mann, it should be noted, won both races.) Upon his second un-retirement, the damage to his right ankle wouldn't allow right-side shifting. But in spite of the gimpy leg, and the feeling that younger racing fans might not know who he was, and that he was out of shape, Hailwood took the notion to race once again at the Isle of Man. The island had lost its Grand Prix status in 1976, when the riders refused to compete for safety reasons. Giacomo Agostini, with 10 TT wins to his credit, had not ridden there since 1972. The first Formula One event was held on the island in 1977, and was won by Hailwood's former competitor Phil Read on a factory Honda.

The decision made, Hailwood put his old friend Ted Macauley to work in England, scouting out the sponsorship possibilities, put himself on a rigorous diet and exercise program, quit drinking, and was back in shape in a few months. The pair went to the island for the amateur Manx Gran Prix in the fall of 1977, where Hailwood rode a TZ750 in practice to familiarize himself with the road, and to test his own abilities. Asked his impression of the Yamaha, he said it was "bloody fearsome. It

The Hailwood and Smart racers are suitably enshrined in the Museo Ducati, which opened in 1998. The Imola bike is the original, on loan from owner Paul Smart. Provenance on the Hailwood bike is more diffuse, the original's parts having been redistributed among other bikes long ago. Tod Rafferty

The Darmah 900 SS came along in 1979, fitted with 40-mm carburetors, five-spoke Campagnolo wheels, and Conti mufflers. This was the sport-touring edition of the 900 Super Sport, though later editions would get downgraded wheels and mufflers. Only about 600 were built through 1983. Guy Webster

nearly threw me off the back." Over the winter Macauley enlisted support from Martini and Rossi, Yamaha, and Sports Motor Cycles, a Ducati dealership in Manchester. Nobby Clark, Hailwood's former mechanic, was then with Kenny Roberts' Yamaha team on the GP circuit, and was released to provide assistance on the island. The game was on.

Friends and colleagues, including John Surtees and Geoff Duke, expressed concern about Hailwood's decision to ride the TT. They knew, despite his comments, that Mike would not make a leisurely tour of the race; that his competitive nature, and his long-standing respect for his fans, would not allow it. His wife, Pauline, was naturally concerned, knowing, as everyone who knew Mike Hailwood knew, that even though he had nothing to prove, Mike the Bike would be incapable of riding below the pace. A few days before the race, Hailwood set off with Macauley in a Rover sedan to refresh his road memory. The pace in civilian traffic was soon too high for Macauley, who politely asked to be dropped at the Highlander Pub for the remainder of Mike's practice session.

To Hailwood's good fortune, in terms of power-to-weight and handling, the NCR Ducati had more in com-mon with his old Manx Norton than the brutal Honda 500-cc four he had ridden in 1967. Plus, brake and suspension technology had advanced considerably in the interim. Unfortunately, six weeks before the TT, the Ducati race bikes were still in Italy. When they finally arrived, Steve Wynne disassembled the engines and installed larger crankpins, added extra keyways in the bevel gears to ensure perfect cam timing, and installed Venolia pistons developed for the Neilson/Schilling Day-tona bike, bringing compression to 11:1. The intake and exhaust ports were gas flowed and polished, and the ignition points replaced with a Lucas Rita electronic sys-tem. Wynne ground off the three short engagement dogs on the fourth gear pinion to solve the traditional popping out of gear problem, and the useless Marzocchi shocks were pitched in favor of Girling gas dampers. With a full tank, the Hailwood Ducati weighed 408 pounds and made 80 horsepower at the rear wheel. Read's Honda made about 100 horsepower.

In practice at the island, Hailwood cut a lap at 111 miles per hour, just over a mile an hour faster than Read's winning average in the Senior a year before, and just shy of the outright record of 112.77

set by Mick Grant on a Kawasaki 750. In the race Hailwood started 50 seconds behind Phil Read's Honda. In the turns, on the mountain, and through the villages, Hailwood could hear the cheers above the thundering resonance of the V-twin. His style remained as it had ever been—compact, knees in, boots grazing the tarmac just before the fairing touched down, lightly, on either side. And smooth, unhurriedly fast as always. Hailwood caught and passed Read at Ballacraine on the second lap, and the cheers went higher as the two raced together for the next two laps, just like the old days until Read's Honda expired on the final lap. Hailwood sped on alone.

And then he won, had made the impossible real. Normally reserved Britons leaped about like children, thumping one another on the back and exclaiming they knew he could do it all along. Fans wearing "Mike the Bike" caps swarmed into the pubs, buying pints for all manner of visiting tourists including Frenchmen. Ted Macauley, beside himself since Mike had taken the lead on the clock in the first lap, was in tears. Even Hailwood, rarely known to let the emotions show, had welled up as he rolled across the line.

The statistics give his victory some perspective. Hailwood's Ducati turned the fastest lap at 110.63 miles per hour, and his race average was 108.51. John

Once again in the muddle of management shuffles in Bologna, it took Ducati more than a year to bring the Mike Hailwood Replica to market. The original 1979 bike-like-Mike's had a fiberglass-covered steel fuel tank and one-piece fairing. The engine and chassis derived from the 900 SS. Guy Webster

Williams' second place Honda trailed by two minutes. Hailwood's time would have put him fifth in the Classic against GP bikes; a few more laps at 110 miles per hour, which he could have done handily, would have put him third. Mike Hailwood's legend needed no further confirmation, he had simply felt keen to race again. But in doing so he engraved the Ducati name indelibly in the old stone archives at the Isle of Man, the original grand theater of international roadracing.

No other man, with the possible exception of Giacomo Agostini, could have imprinted Ducati with a more lustrous seal of authenticity. Fifteen years later, Agostini would say, "The island is one of the best for driving, but you have to think about the life . . . about the safety, because the Isle of Man is really dangerous. But for driving, it's the most pleasure you can have with a motorbike." The pleasure. That's what Mike Hailwood got from racing on the island, and what he gave the fans, the sponsors, and the manufacturers for whom he rode. The pleasure of his company, and his grace. Irish racer and friend Tommy Robb is quoted on the cover of Christopher Hilton's fine biography, *A Man Called Mike,* "I'm proud to say I raced with Mike Hailwood . . . I was beaten by Mike Hailwood."

Phil Read, who may have taken less pride in defeat, admitted, "He was a master, and sporting with it as well. You felt that you could race shoulder to shoulder with Mike and he wouldn't take any unfair advantage. He'd beat you by absolute ability."

And from Phil Schilling: "Hailwood took so little out of motorcycling and gave so much back. He gave life to racing's impossible dream; that success could come early and develop as naturally as growing up. He showed that awesome talent, tied to a man confident of his own self-worth and comfortable with himself, would not lead to consuming egotism. He verified the secret hope of all men aging: that time could not gut the talent and force of youth. He demonstrated that motorcycle racing could be heroic theater. Outside motorcycle circles he was widely recognized as a winner, and motorcyclists everywhere shared in that recognition. This man at ease with himself reassured this sport of its own importance. But most of all he gave motorcycling his majesty."

In 1979, Hailwood returned to the island and won the Senior event on a Suzuki RGB 500, setting a new class record at 114 miles per hour, three seconds shy of the absolute record. Mike Hailwood, 40, and his daugh-ter Michelle, 9, died in an automobile accident in England in March 1981.

Shuffling to Varese

In Bologna, Ducati was no better prepared to exploit the Isle of Man win than it had been for Imola in 1972. Little thought had apparently been given to the possibility that Hailwood might actually win at the Isle of Man. Racing had been largely delegated to NCR, with the coordination of Franco Farne and a few chronic racing junkies at the factory, and the focus was almost exclusively on endurance events.

The more immediate task at hand was to bring the completely new Pantah to market, to further civilianize the 900 SS, introduce the Darmah SS, and get the Mike Hailwood Replica on the market. Meanwhile, the new government-appointed group of regulators had looked at Ducati's deficit, now in the tens of millions (dollars, not lira), and said, Please would you build the motorcycles many people will buy? To which we can only imagine Taglioni replying, but of course, whatever you wish, and returning to his drawing board. In fact, the plans for the Pantah engine had been drafted several years earlier, and the maestro knew that it would satisfy the need for a more cost-effective power plant.

The master of desmodromics had been with Ducati for 25 years, and was entering his final phase as head of design and production. EFIM, the Ducati management group, had effectively eliminated direct racing involvement by the factory, and NCR had become the official conduit for competition customers. Now a new organization, the Rome-based VM group, was appointed to direct the fortunes of Ducati Meccanica. The new management put considerable emphasis on converting a portion of the Bologna plant for the production of industrial diesel engines, their primary product. This postponed the introduction of the Pantah, but likewise allowed time to finally bring the Mike Hailwood Replica (MHR) on line and to tinker and fiddle with the Darmah. Together these models would comprise the final incarnations of the 900 SS, and the last examples of the bevel-drive V-twin introduced in 1971.

As Ducati's stylish exemplar of sporting civility, the Darmah was in numerical terms the most successful of the bevel twins. The outlines penned by Leo Tartarini were shifting from the 1960s swoopiness to more traditional shapes, as the tail section tucked in and the exaggerated stripe went away. As the electric-start 900

SS for the slightly less sporting gentleman, the Darmah filled the market category that had eluded Ducati so often. The sport-touring segment was expanding, only partially served by the Japanese builders and eager for motorcycles that handled, went fast, and didn't require an hour of work for an hour of riding. And that were affordable. The last vestige of incivility, the kickstarter, was gone in 1979, and the Darmah became Marzocchi suspended at both ends. The color choices were red and white or black and gold. In a final tribute to the original 750 SS, and to

use up the fairings still on the shelf, the Darmah SS appeared in 1979 with the half fairing and two-tone blue paint scheme.

The 900 Super Sport was still in production, and reached its one-year peak of 1,205 machines in 1981. But by then it was being outstripped by the Hailwood Replica, which had been delayed for nearly two years. The MHR replicated more form than function; the red, green, and white livery left little doubt about its national origin, but the underpinnings were stock 900 SS engine and running gear. The NCR-styled fiber-

Last of the bevel-drives, the Mike Hailwood Replica Mille was offered in 1984. About 1,100 of the 973-cc models were built in a two-year period. The final edition was based on the 900 S2, with an electric starter and hydraulic clutch. With the final takeover by Cagiva, the production of MHRs was discontinued. Guy Webster

glass tank was merely a cover for the steel item underneath. And the one-piece fairing made routine maintenance more of a chore.

The early MHRs arrived with 40-mm carburetors and Conti mufflers, which did go some little way to suggest a serious sportster. The instrumentation and switchgear derived from the Darmah, but the electric starter didn't make the trip. The Speedline cast wheels carried Brembo calipers front and rear, and both rims were 18-inch. In 1980 a larger fuel tank eliminated the cosmetic cover, and the fairing became a three-piece item. The Contis gave way to Silentium mufflers in 1981, and side panels appeared on the following year's model. In 1983 the MHR got the complete body massage with new fairing, side panels, tail section, and fenders.

The final sport rendition of the Darmah, the 900 S2, appeared in 1983 to lukewarm reviews. The S2 was offered with kick or electric start and wore a new half fairing and tail section. Designed to replace the 900 SS, and fit between the Darmah and the MHR, the 900 S2 was widely perceived as a parts-bin special that was neither fish nor cheesecake. The engine was subsequently enlarged to 973-cc, and the bike designated the Mille S2, which was effectively the final iteration of the 900 SS. Both the MHR and the S2 would make the corporate transition into the Cagiva organization, and a few hundred Replicas were sold in 1985 and 1986.

Even though the MHR was a largely cosmetic version of the legendary racer, the imagery worked at least to prolong the production of bevel twins a few years longer—a just and worthy cause. For some of the congenital Ducatisti, those who had grown up with the company, who had admired the singles and rhapsodized over the twins, the next era would be less engaging. The Pantah's "rubber band" engine would never replace the lovely harmony of perfectly shimmed bevel gears spinning away and the bass counterpoint of Conti megaphones drumming across the landscape. Some elitism was at work, perhaps, tinged with a measure of nostalgia. Whatever the case, in the 1980s they wouldn't make 'em like they used to.

CHAPTER 5

The Cagiva Complex

1980-1990

Despite the publicity boost from Hailwood's Isle of Man victory, Ducati faced a sea of troubles as the decade turned; the tardiness in bringing the MHR to market was a minor inconvenience compared to the gathering forces from both within the company and those well outside its control.

Taglioni had already recognized the impending need for a quieter and more cost-effective engine, in terms of both parts and labor. The bevel-drive twins were expensive on both counts, and maintaining the design would make the motorcycles too costly to build or buy. The new Pantah V-twin retained the 90-degree engine with desmo valve gear, but featured belt-driven cams in lieu of the bevel-drive towers. Although the change elicited a collective moan among the traditional Ducatisti, the efficiency, weight savings, quiet operation, and simplified manufacture made the belts a logical choice for an all-new design.

The original Pantah prototype of 1977 derived from the double overhead-cam, four-valve, 500-cc racing engine built by the outside firm of Armaroli in 1973. The experimental heads and barrels had been grafted to the bevel-drive, narrow-sump cases, and fitted in the original Seeley frame. The engine carried its toothed belts on the left side, and the rear cylinder exhaust port was in the back. While the performance of the four-valve racing heads didn't show marked improvement over the bevel-drive two-valvers of the Pantah, the rubber belts proved quite durable under racing conditions. And valve timing suffered no loss in accuracy.

The Pantah represented a new direction for Ducati.

The Pantah engine had little in common with the previous Ducati V-twins, beyond the 90-degree layout and desmo valves. The electric starter was tucked under the front cylinder, adjacent to the new automotive-style cartridge oil filter. A new transmission and hydraulic clutch came with the 600. Tod Rafferty

PANTAH 600 TL

Impianto frenante con tre freni a disco
Braking system with 3 discs

Cruscotto con strumentazione
Dash-board

The 600 TL was conceived as the touring version of the Pantah, and the handlebar/footpeg relationship afforded a more upright riding position. The TL was absent the SL's hydraulic clutch. A fleet of white 600 TLs was purchased for urban patrol by the Bologna police department.

The new cylinder bores were coated with silicon-carbon particles for heat conductivity and durability, though the process eliminated the option of over-boring them. The one-piece forged crankshaft was supported by ball-bearing mains, and the two-piece rods had plain-bearing big ends, requiring a high-pressure lubrication system. The Pantah's front cylinder was offset to the right, opposite of the bevel-drive layout, and a new transmission design meant the crankshaft spun "forward" rather than "backward" as had the earlier engines.

Driven by helical spur gears on the left side, the cam-driveshaft crossed to the right at the crotch of the V. Pulleys at its end drove the two toothed belts connected to the overhead cams. The belts ran below a fixed pulley on the way up and an adjustable one on the way back. Ducati specified changing the belts at 12,500 miles, though it was widely considered a conservative figure posted to establish the belts' durability under real-world use.

The frame abandoned the Seeley style for a ladder-type trellis arrangement. The engine hung from six mounting tabs, and the swingarm spindle passed through the rear of the crankcase, its bushings lubricated by engine oil. While not possessed of the rigidity of the earlier twin frame, the Pantah cage was adequate for the weight and power of the 500-cc engine, and testers reported that handling was traditional Ducati-agile. The riding position was definitely more sporting than tourist, and too close to the racing crouch for most American riders. The combined seat-handlebar-footpeg configuration was fine for short sprints on back roads, but for either long hauls on the freeway or putting about town, the Pantah induced stiff necks, sore wrists, and numb butts.

With 57 inches of wheelbase, and a 30.5-degree steering head angle, the Pantah provided traditional Ducati stability with characteristic slow steering. A new generation of American sport riders was growing more accustomed to the quicker flickery of Japanese middleweights, most prominent among them the Kawasaki GPz, which dove into turns almost instinctively. The Pantah, however, paid benefits in ground clearance and rock-steady behavior in high-speed curves; the Marzocchi suspension was, again in the Italian tradition, firm but untroubled by pavement irregularities at speed.

When the prototype Pantah appeared in late 1977, the Tartarini bodywork had been lifted directly from the late and unlamented 350/500 vertical twin. The tank and seat looked better on the new machine and may have become production bodywork, until someone realized that the lack of distinction between the two was unlikely to help the sales figures. So Tartarini was commissioned to restyle the Pantah, and once again the malicious styling gargoyle arose from the wine cellar and fixed its baleful glare on Bologna. The show model, in all fairness, wore simply a modified version of the NCR seat and tank and a full fairing based on the racing-kit version from the 900 SS. The tank and tail section were too large for the rest of the motorcycle, but the overall look was stylish cafe racer.

The production bodywork, however, featured a modified version of the MHR-style seat/tail section, 5.5-gallon fuel tank, and a half fairing. Once again the persistent design trend substituted sharp edges and sculpted creases for the traditional round and flowing shapes, and once again the styling was received with a collective yawn. (The British motopress expressed fondness for the form, though it should be remembered that they tend to get excited when the sun shines.)

The fairing was another indication that function had been subordinated to form, with what could have been unsettling results on the road. The leading edge of the fairing ran at about 45 degrees from the headlight to the apex of the cylinders; the flat leading surface on the bottom amounted to some 2 square feet of nonadjustable aileron. At speed on an uphill grade, and more dramatically at the crest of a hill, the subsequent aerodynamic lift would do a dance with the steering

Although it was unlikely that any civilian Pantah rider would reach the speed, under the right conditions, to fly off into the great unknown, the problem got fixed. In one of those examples where racing actually does improve the breed, the fairing was redesigned with a more shallow angle of attack. The new shroud featured a chin spoiler, for the opposite of lift, and an enlarged air scoop extending to the base of the headlight, which helped cool the rear cylinder. The new model, made of ABS plastic rather than fiberglass, eliminated the potential handling problem, but few found the fairing attractive. Nonetheless, the rocket boy styling, which would later be institutionalized by Japanese designers, was here to stay. Some would blame the influence of American comic

Last of the Pantahs were the 650 SL models, built from 1984 to 1986. This engine met the homologation requirements for Formula Two racing, where Ducati planned to make its next competition imprint. The same engine would be used in the Cagiva model called the Alazzura. Guy Webster

The first 600-cc racing Pantahs were developed concurrently with the road models and became available in 1980. Factory machines had NCR bodywork with full fairing, while kitted privateer models wore a half fairing based on the street model's. Both got the 2-into-1 exhaust system.

books and an adolescent fascination with jet fighter planes.

And the Pantah was, in fact, geared for the moon. First gear was tall enough for better than 50 miles per hour and required plenty of clutch slippage to get under way; fortunately the wet clutch was a stout unit. Unfortunately, a he-man grip was required to disengage the multiple plates and could turn a short ride into a forearm-building workout. Fifth gear was effectively an overdrive, since with stock carburetion and mufflers the Pantah registered higher top speed (115 miles per hour) in fourth. In its 1981 test of the 500, *Cycle* found the Pantah would pull to 8,000 rpm in fifth only after a long tucked-in run on a flat and windless road. So with a claimed 46 horsepower at 8,500 rpm, tall gearing, and a curb weight of 440 pounds, the Pantah 500 was wheezing against the class-leading Kawasaki GPz 550. Still, the Pantah was quick for a 500-cc twin, and the potential for more performance was apparent.

Finally, two other elements conspired against the Pantah's success. The first was its price of $4,500, a stupefying $1,800 more than a GPz 550. The Kawasaki may have been 30 pounds heavier, but it was also quicker, faster, more comfortable, and dead-nuts reliable. The knockout punch came when the overall motorcycle market in America, which had been declining for several years, went flat as an iron rail just as the Pantah arrrived.

Rubber-Drive Racers

Taglioni was now less insulated from the demands of the market and found himself increasingly occupied with assistant engineers installed by the new manage-

The Pantah TT2 was ready for the 1981 racing season. About 30 racers were built in the first run, fitted with 40-mm Dell'Orto carburetors and 16-inch wheels. Rated at 78 horsepower at 10,500 rpm, and about 320 pounds race-ready, the TT2 was one speedy Gonzales. This bike is owned by Daniele Casolari. Tod Rafferty

ment. But racing remained well within imagination; despite the ongoing managerial shuffle in Bologna and the economic vicissitudes of the motorcycle market, Ducati would always race. Development of the racing Pantah, called the TT, was under parallel construction at NCR as a 600-cc machine. The factory version had aggressive cams, a two-into-one exhaust system, and made 70 horsepower at 9,800 rpm. The Marzocchi fork wore magnesium sliders, the Brembo brakes grabbed drilled rotors, and the cast-alloy wheels were shod with Michelin slicks. The kitted rendition available to privateers carried the half fairing of the road model.

Once again it was left to Sports Motor Cycles of England to prove the Pantah's possibilities at the Isle of Man. Provided a well-used test engine by the factory, Sports Motor Cycles (SMC) modified a production street frame and fitted Koni shocks and Dymag wheels. With British rider Tony Rutter aboard, the Pantah took the Formula Two class in 1981 with a race average just shy of 102 miles per hour, and a lap record of 103.5. Ducati, understandably pleased with the result, furnished Rutter with one of the five factory TT2 racers built for the Italian championship. He went on to win the title and repeat the feat the next three years running. Then 40 years old, Tony Rutter was an accomplished short-circuit rider and an Isle of Man veteran, having won the Junior TT on Yamaha in 1973 and 1974. In winning the 1982 Formula Two race on the TT2, Rutter put in a 109.27–mile per hour lap on the island, with an average that would have put him third in the 1,000-cc Formula One event.

The original Pantah TT had served to reveal the weak points of the trellis frame, which led to the development of the TT2. The real racer got a Verlicchi chrome-moly frame (18 pounds with swingarm), Paioli monoshock, and Campagnolo wheels; the wheelbase measured 55 inches. The engine received more serious cams, larger intake ports and valves, and 41-mm Dell'Orto carbs, with the compression ratio up to 10.4:1. The stock Pantah cases held a dry clutch with hydraulic actuation and a magnesium cover. The TT2 made close to 80 horsepower and weighed only 300 pounds ready to race. The 583-cc belt-cammer developed serious urge from 6,000 to 11,000 rpm, good for about 145 miles per hour, and could flat belittle many 750-cc and Open-class machines. Factory rider Walter Cussigh, who pioneered the 16-front wheel with fat rubber, won the Italian Formula Two National Championship in 1981.

Ducati again collaborated with Sports Motor Cycles of Manchester to race in Formula Two at the Isle of Man. British veteran Tony Rutter had taken the shop's road-based special to victory on the island in 1981, which leveraged the real-racer gear from Bologna for the following year.

A half-dozen factory TT2s were built for the Italian national championship series in 1981. The engines had a dry clutch in a magnesium case, desmo valves disposed at 60 degrees, 10.4:1 compression, a five-speed gearbox, Verlicchi frame, Marzocchi suspension, and 16-inch Campagnolo wheels.

Jimmy Adamo at speed. With Reno Leoni and Adamo campaigning Ducati twins in the United States, Bologna's racing image was maintained through another phase of shifting managements and priorities in Italy. Tom Riles

The civilian Pantah 600 SL also appeared in 1981, with a hydraulic clutch and the aforementioned new fairing. In 1982 the SL wore a Paioli rather than Marzocchi fork, with slightly larger brake rotors and the Brembo calipers moved behind the fork legs. A touring version, the 600 TL, appeared in 1983 with a headlight fairing and full-length, louvered side panels from the toaster-oven school of design. The 350 XL was the economy model, and the 500 SL remained in production. In 1984 the engine was stroked to produce the 650 SL and supply new owner Cagiva the engine for the Alazzurra and 650 SS models, Pantahs by other names.

While the Pantah engine design would carry the Ducati marque on through the Cagiva years, and eventually into Superbike racing history, the model itself was largely unsuccessful in the United States. In its next iteration, as the 750-cc F1, Ducati would start to regain some lost ground, but the Bolognese renaissance would proceed without the services of Berliner Motors as the U.S. importer. The New Jersey firm suspended operation in 1983, and Ducati imports slowed to a trickle as the scramble ensued to establish a new distributorship. But the Pantah engine, Taglioni's "compromise" design of the mid-1970s, would emerge to carry the Ducati banner to new heights. In the meantime, importation of Ducatis in the States dribbled down to a complete stop in 1984.

Despite the virtual absence of an official Ducati presence in the United States in the mid-1980s, the team of tuner Reno Leoni and rider Jimmy Adamo, and privateers such as Sydney and Malcolm Tunstall, Dale Newton, and Paul Ritter, maintained Bologna's position on American racetracks. U.S. Superbike racing had changed comprehensively since the California Hot Rod was retired in 1978. The rules had been relaxed to permit all manner of nonproduction equipment, and the Japanese fours, in addition to their massive horsepower, had been greatly massaged in the handling department. The twins—BMW, Harley, Moto Guzzi, and Ducati—were relegated to the Battle of the Twins class, making its official AMA-sanctioned debut at Daytona in 1981.

Reno Leoni, former Ducati test rider, had been sent from Bologna to work with the Berliners in 1965. He soon changed the spelling of his first name so Americans would stop calling him Rhino, and built fast and reliable 250 and 350 Desmos for riders George Rockett and Frank Camillieri on the East Coast, both of whom did well. Running a 42-mm carburetor, the 350 could stick with the Yamaha TD1B up to 110 miles per hour, and easily dispatch the British bikes in the turns.

With the help of Taglioni and Franco Farne, Leoni became the unofficial racing director for Ducati in the United States. Not a high-salary position by any means, but Leoni had a distinct advantage given Ducati's racing heritage: U.S. production roadracing was in the fledgling stages, and few riders or tuners had much experience with the form. Given the successes of Leoni's swift singles, American-style horsepower obviously wasn't the paramount issue.

Ten years later Leoni built a Moto Guzzi racer to contest the newly popular format called Superbike racing. Instituted as a privateer division for production machines, distinct from expensive factory racing efforts, Superbikes initially attracted a healthy variety of builders and tuners of Japanese fours and European and American twins. On the East Coast, Mike Baldwin blistered the fours on Leoni's Guzzi, and in 1978 the pair campaigned a similarly specialized Ducati/NCR 750 Desmo. By now, only a year after the Neilson/Schilling Daytona win, the sophistication level in Superbike racing had made a significant leap. More special parts—suspension, swingarms, carburetors, cams, valves, pistons—had appeared, and the old gentleman's agreement to ignore creative rule-bending was showing some strain.

At the inaugural Battle of the Twins race at Daytona in 1980, the Leoni/Adamo Ducati 900 ran 157 miles per hour. At the Loudon AMA race later that year, warned

that the Ducati would be protested, Mike Baldwin finished second to Wes Cooley's Yoshimura Suzuki even though the Ducati had the measure of the four. The protest was filed anyway, and Leoni's Ducati was disqualified for an illegal spin-on oil filter.

Arbitrary rules notwithstanding, the big twins were steadily losing ground to the four-cylinder onslaught, and were subordinated to the Battle of the Twins class. Here the Leoni/Adamo Ducati was a genuine overdog and dominated the division. In 1983, the AMA again changed the Superbike formula, dropping the open class rules and limiting four-cylinders to 750-cc. Twins kept the original 1,000-cc limit, but even with the added displacement, Ducati—let alone Leoni—couldn't hope to match the raging technological flood and huge budgets the Japanese factories poured into AMA Superbike.

Although the displacement margin seemed the only way to keep any twins in Superbike racing, the formula

didn't attract immediate support from either camp. And by letting the factories through the door, the AMA had effectively excluded privateers from making the podium. With Honda, Kawasaki, and Suzuki ready to do battle for the minds and hearts of American sport riders, even a 275-cc displacement bonus was unlikely to put the Ducati twin on an even footing. And Ducati, then in the throes of its transmogrification from state-owned enterprise to privately held Cagiva engine supplier, was in no position to field a state-of-the-art racing twin. But the possibilities were not lost on the boys in Bologna, or several of the Stateside Ducatisti. However, the initial task at hand was to fulfill the mandate of the new management, in the persons of Giancarlo and Claudio Castiglioni.

The Cagiva Conglomeration

Harley-Davidson had bought half-interest in Aeronautica Macchi in 1960 and sold both its two- and four-

Adamo practiced on a TT2 at Daytona in 1983 but rode the bigger bevel-drive in the race. The Battle of the Twins had attracted the big iron from Harley, who put dirt-tracker Jay Springsteen on an XR 1000 with a dated chassis and fairing. He won the race and Adamo was second. **Tom Riles**

The first of the Cagiva Elefant herd were the 600-cc Pantah-engine models of 1984, followed by a 650 version a year later. The 750 Elefant arrived in 1987, after considerable testing in the Paris-Dakar rally. Cagiva won the event in 1990 with Edi Orioli on a 900-cc Elefant.

England where the sun happened to be shining. The motorsports press was all atwitter, and members quickly quit their offices for the pubs where the possible passing of Ducati was lamented at length over many pints.

Their Italian counterparts exhibited little excitement. Even at Ducati itself, the transition was generally welcomed as an opportunity to devote more attention, and perhaps more financing, to the development of the new V-twin. In fact, Ducati had started as an engine supplier in the 1950s, and even when the company later moved to complete machines, most of the non-engine components came from outside contractors. So the Cagiva connection was not unwelcome in Bologna. Plus, the Castiglioni brothers, in true Italian fashion, also expressed keen interest in racing motorcycles, although roadracing, as it turned out, was not at the top of their list.

The early 1980s were witness to a spike of growth for dual-purpose motorcycles, what had formerly been broadly classified as street-legal enduro bikes. The Paris-Dakar Rally, which sounds like a jolly-good sporting romp in the desert but was actually a 3,000-mile exercise in pain, desperation, and brutal exhaustion, had reached the phase of popular fashion. BMW had introduced its R80 G/S "adventure-tourer" in 1980, and Frenchman Herbert Auriol rode one to win the daunting desert dash in 1981 and again in 1983. The Bavarian battlewagon generated a glut of urban panzers, all tall, loud, and dressed in designer lederhosen. The off-road roadster became the European equivalent of a custom cruiser in the United States; while the boulevard scrambler was short on comfort and conveniences, it was likewise swift and stable on the mountain roads and back streets.

The brothers Castiglioni were understandably keen to build a Cagiva/Ducati multipurpose assault vehicle and had a prototype on display at the Milan show in the fall of 1983. Owing to the flexible nature of Italian business agreements, the Elefant didn't appear in any numbers until the middle of 1986. Cagiva hired double-winner Auriol to ride Paris-Dakar, but BMW had signed ex-world motocross champ Gaston Rahier to ride the G/S and won again.

In the interim, Ducati was faced with the disposition of the remaining inventory of bevel-drive parts. The agreement with Cagiva seemed subject to revision on a monthly basis, and until the final contract was sealed, Ducati would continue to produce the 900, and subsequently 1,000, S2 and MHR, the 600TT and 750 Corsa, until the supply of components was consumed. Then

stroke singles in the United States. The overhead-valve Sprint had some success as a dual-purpose machine and dirt-track racer, but was later eclipsed by Japanese bikes. Italian star Renzo Pasolini was third in the 1966 world roadracing championship on the 350, and Kel Carruthers came second on one at the Isle of Man in 1969. Italy's Walter Villa won the world 250-cc title on the Aermacchi two-stroke twin from 1974 to 1976, adding the 350 class the final year.

Giancarlo and Claudio Castiglioni bought Aermacchi from Harley-Davidson in 1978. Their company name, Cagiva, derived from the combined first syllables of their surname, their father's name, Giovanni, and their hometown of Varese, just north of Milan. The lads had done well in the family hardware manufacturing business, and both had long nurtured the desire to build their own motorcycles. They reached an agreement with the state's VM Group in 1983, and Ducati became a Cagiva engine supplier while continuing to build its own machines, albeit in limited numbers.

The announcement created instant rumors of Ducati's imminent demise, and had a serious impact in

Ducati would build engines exclusively for Cagiva. By 1985 the Castiglionis wearied of dealing through the Italian government's VM Group and bought Ducati outright for some $5 million. Cagiva would expand quickly, acquiring Moto Morini and Husqvarna in 1986.

Meanwhile, back in Bologna, the new Ducati engineering staff made ready the final edition of the bevel-drive twin. Massimo Bordi had joined Ducati in 1978 and worked with Taglioni on the final edition of the Mike Hailwood Replica, the Mille. Among several associate engineers, Bordi soon emerged as the successor to the grand master of desmodromics and was appointed technical director in 1982. The pair developed the final editions of the bevel-drive desmos, the 1000 MHR and S2.

Consideration was given to production of an updated V-4 engine, but the project was shelved for both cost and ideological reasons. Taglioni wanted to build the four, while Bordi campaigned forcefully for an updated V-twin based on the Pantah engine. His 1975 engineering thesis had been on the design for a desmodromic four-valve cylinder head. A fan of the British Cosworth racing V-8 then dominating GP auto racing, Bordi submitted that there was considerable untapped potential still lurking in the V-twin. Dr. Taglioni disagreed, but youth and persistence prevailed.

The Pantah had proven the economic and performance usefulness of the one-piece crankshaft with plain rod bearings, and adapting them to the bevel-drive engines helped make the 1000 MHR and S2 more cost-effective. The hydraulic clutch, stronger transmission, and Nikasil-coated cylinders added another measure of durability. Crankpin diameter on these final bevel-twins increased from 38 to 45 mm, and displacement with 88-mm bore and 80-mm stroke came out to 972 cc. With larger valves and 9.5:1 compression, the engine made 80 horsepower at 7,000 rpm in legal street trim. According to the judicious research of Ian Falloon in his book *Ducati Super Sport,* only 171 of the 1000 S2 were manufactured, and 1,112 of the final MHR models, the last few hundred offered in 1986.

Taglioni's Final Touch

With Ducati facing an uncertain but seemingly more civilized future, it was entirely appropriate that the last pre-Cagiva model would be the decidedly uncivilized F1. Fabio Taglioni quite probably recognized that this would represent his final design and that it would be a fitting tribute to the original TT1 ridden by Mike Hailwood in 1978.

The 650 SL engine was bored to 88-mm and retained the 61.5-mm stroke, producing a well-oversquare and rev-happy configuration. While the engine made only about 60 horsepower in its original form, the F1 was good for 127 miles per hour. Of course the F1 devolved from the TT2, not the MHR, and was closer to a genuine race replica than the bevel-drive version. The first Pantah TT1 was a 750-cc rendition of the TT2, with the adoption of rising-rate rear suspension. Leoni had built a stinky fast 700-cc version for Jimmy Adamo, and John Williams rode a kitted 750 to a BOTT victory at Laguna Seca in 1984.

The factory edition was built specifically for European endurance racing, chosen as the best testing ground and showcase for the new twin. Plus, the displacement limit had been reduced from 1,000 to 750 cc, diluting the advantage of the Japanese fours.

The TT1, at 310 pounds wet, with an electric starter, made 94 horsepower at 10,000 rpm, but the racing engines suffered valve seat and guide failure under such stresses. By now the rumors of a desmodromic four-valve head had sparked the public's imagination.

While not achieving its predecessor's racing success, the TT1 led directly to the production of the civilian F1 Replica in 1985. With smaller valves and a

In standard dual-sport trim the 900 Elefant was called the 900E in the United States. The go-almost-anywhere models became the most popular Cagiva-badged machines around the world. The final example of the series, called the Gran Canyon, lasted beyond the separation of Ducati and Cagiva.

The 750-cc TT1 led eventually to the development of a road version, the F1. The racing frame was modified for street equipment, but the wheelbase remained at 55 inches. The F1 was much closer to being a genuine race-replica than the MHR series had been, making it a hard-edged street rod. Guy Webster

The F1 Montjuich, built to commemorate the 1983 24-Hour victory, was an upscale limited edition for 1986. Hot cams, 40-mm carburetors, a racing exhaust, better suspension, and Marvic composite wheels made the Montjuich the lightest and fastest of the F1 series. Guy Webster

9,000-rpm redline, the production engine made about 80 horsepower and showed good reliability. The well-tri-angulated Verlicchi trestle frame was modified and grafted to the Pantah rear section, including a steel-tube swingarm in lieu of the racer's box-section aluminum unit. Some 60 pounds heavier than the racer, with about 60 horses at the rear wheel, the F1 was scorned by the purists as a seriously diluted replica. Still, it was a 135-miles per hour machine off the floor—with an engine that promised more to come and some dispensable weight.

What the TT2 had displayed, and by extension the F1 confirmed, was how compact a motorcycle could be built around a 90-degree V-twin. With the Cagiva incorporation came the wherewithal to build out the remaining stock of Ducati parts, since the new owners had several motorcycles of their own in mind and wished to get on with it.

Thus some 2,200 F1s were built between 1985 and 1987, including a few hundred special editions. The Santa Monica (after the raceway at Misano), Laguna Seca, and Montjuich all got 40-mm rather than 36-mm carburetors, larger valves, higher compression, and performance exhaust systems. The Laguna Seca honored the 1986 BOTT victory there of Marco Lucchinelli, who had been world 500-cc GP champion for Suzuki in 1981.

The Montjuich celebrated Ducati's long history of accomplishment in the 24 Hours of Barcelona. More robust cams, Japanese electronic ignition, and a racing exhaust system brought the Montjuich closer to a racer replica. The running gear was upgraded with an aluminum

Marco Lucchinelli won the 1986 Daytona Battle of the Twins on the factory TT1, and took the Formula One championship race at Misano. This racer had rising rate rear suspension, and more power, less weight, and improved brakes. "Lucky" won Daytona again in 1987 on the prototype 851. Walther Scagliarini

swingarm, better shock absorber, wide 16-inch Marvic wheels, and four-piston Brembo racing brakes. At 385 pounds and about 70 rear-wheel horsepower, the Montjuich was good for 136 miles per hour. Only 200 each of the Laguna Seca and Montjuich were produced, before emphasis shifted to the 750 Paso and Elefant as Cagiva moved to define and address new market segments. That effort would include an American-style cruiser.

The strength of the Castiglionis' resolve was apparent at Imola in 1985, when they fielded two 500-cc two-stroke GP bikes and two Ducati F1s. The pilots were Marco Lucchinelli and Virginio Ferrari, 1982 World 500-cc GP champion on Suzuki. Two national heros, at Ducati's home track, prepared to take on the substantial might of the factory teams of the Japanese. Lucchinelli won the Formula One race at Misano in 1986, and the Daytona BOTT event as well. *Cycle World* executive editor Steve Anderson took the Montjuich to victory in the resurrected 140-mile La Carrera roadrace, run on the Baja peninsula between Ensenada and San Felipe. So the F1 had gone quite some distances, at brisk speeds, to reinforce Ducati's racing traditions just as the company was enveloped in a critically transitional phase.

That remarkable curtain call created lasting currency that continued through the release of the first

The 750 Paso was the distinctive signal that Cagiva was ready for something completely different. Named in memory of racer Renzo Pasolini, the fully-enclosed machine designed by Massimo Tamburini departed from Ducati models in chassis design and construction as well as bodywork.

Cagiva-Ducati collaboration, the Paso 750. Designed by Massimo Tamburini, co-founder of Bimota, and Massimo Bordi, the Paso was a distinct departure from the Ducati style. As Cagiva had done with the Elefant, the rear head was reversed to accommodate a single Weber two-barrel carburetor feeding both cylinders. The carburetor and its accompanying airbox were employed to meet tightening emission and noise regulations in the United States, also the rationale for the whisper-note Silentium mufflers. The engine also carried a new 14-plate dry clutch.

But the all-enclosing bodywork bespoke Bimota, and was in fact Tamburini's vision of the Italian sport for the masses. Gone was the trademark Ducati trellis frame, in its stead a full-cradle unit of box-section steel tubing. The lower tubes could be unbolted for engine service, and the rear cylinder was removable with the engine in the frame—an improvement over the trellis-framed models. The steering head was set at 25 degrees, with 4 inches of trail, and the wheelbase went out to 57 inches, shifting weight bias to the front wheel.

The Marzocchi M1 fork featured divided damping duties; the left leg took care of the fixed compression stroke, the right leg handled the variable rebound, with an external adjustment at axle level. In concert with the Marzocchi rising-rate rear suspension and chubby 16-inch Pirelli radial tires, the Paso handled nicely in the sweepers and the twisties and was relatively comfortable. The civilizing factor again, but to good effect since the Paso targeted the sport-touring rider rather than the gonzo street racer.

But once again, the fashion maven and raving sportrider were seldom one and the same customer. The notion of fully enclosed motorcycles was just beginning to come into vogue. Bimota's db1 (also a Tamburini design) foreshadowed Ducati's entry and Honda's 600 Hurricane (aka CBR600) followed it a few months later. The avant-garde styling was not without its detractors, however, especially among the traditional Ducatisti, accustomed to the open-air styling of the Paso's trellis-framed predecessors. The Paso was aerodynamically superior to most enclosed motorcycles, and arguably an aesthetic advancement as well.

And riders bought them in numbers sufficient to keep the Paso in production for seven years, which is hardly short term on an Italian timepiece. So the Paso did establish the existence of the niche for super-streamliners and set good standards for their execution.

In 1989, Ducati abandoned the air-cooled 750 in the Paso, replacing it with a new V-twin loosely based on the new 851 Superbike engine. Combining the 851's

The second-generation Paso 906 in 1989 had a water-cooled engine but was still hobbled by the single Weber carburetor. The 904-cc engine brought more urge and a six-speed transmission. The 906 was 20 pounds heavier than the Paso 750, and was still fitted with 16-inch wheels.

Previews of the desmoquattro appeared in Italy in 1986. Engineers Massimo Bordi and Luigi Mendoli worked with Weber-Marelli to refine the integrated ignition/fuel injection system, and Marco Lucchinelli conducted testing in the Italian national championship events.

The Indiana cruised in from the Midwestern plains, via Hollywood. Some European and Japanese renderings of American-style motorcycles had come to be characterized in the United States as amusing examples of occasional comic relief. That tradition was firmly upheld by the Ducati Indiana.

92-mm bore with a 68-mm stroke (up 4 mm from the Superbike) gave the new power plant an actual displacement of 904 cc. Now a six-speed, the new model was dubbed the 906. Although it retained the 750's single overhead-cam head design and dual-throat Weber carburetor, the 906 engine was liquid-cooled, so instead of the fairing lettering with *Controlled Air Flow,* the new model read *Liquid Cooled.* This sort of letterbox labeling, apparently adopted from the Japanese, was fortunately discontinued on the final Pasos.

For 1991 and its almost final variant, the Paso exchanged its model name for an alphanumeric designation, the 907 IE, for its Marelli-Weber electronic fuel injection. The low-range stumbles of the earlier carbureted models were gone, and the 907 made slightly more horsepower. Seventeen-inch wheels became standard, and four-piston calipers embraced larger full-floating front brake rotors. In 1992, last of the breed, the 907 got top-shelf Brembo Gold Line brakes at both ends, and yet again larger rotors on the front. The new windscreen incorporated a duct to reduce turbulence behind the fairing.

Finally, even some who found it difficult to pass on the Paso styling were dissuaded by its price, which went from $6,400 in 1987 ($2,400 more than a Honda 600 Hurricane) to $8,800 in 1991 ($1,800 above the Honda CBR 1000F). While Ducatis had indeed been rendered more civil with the Cagiva refurbish, Japanese motorcycles had made commensurate advances in handling, comfort, and applicable horsepower. Not to mention swoopy bodywork. The Italians were not unaccustomed

to working from a price disadvantage, but the Honda Hurricane had more than price on its side. With dual overhead cams and four valves per cylinder, the 600-cc four made 67 horsepower at 10,500 rpm, weighed 45 pounds less than the Paso, and was nearly a full second quicker in the quarter-mile. The Paso held the cards in suspension compliance and high-speed cornering stability, and the romantic trappings of Italian design. Most of the practical and nearly all of the frugal Yanks had an easy buying choice.

While the Paso may have been slightly ahead of its time stylistically, it was off the pace in terms of performance technology. Seamless carburetion, blazing acceleration, and decent suspension had become minimum standard requirements for the majority of U.S. sporting riders by the mid-1980s. And the Japanese continued to elevate the norms for fit and finish. The Paso may not have made the measure on some counts, but it signaled Cagiva's intent to run with the larger dogs. Perhaps most importantly, underneath it was still a Ducati V-twin.

Elephants in Indiana

If the Paso had suprised the traditional Ducatisti, the Indiana was a cavallo of a whole 'nother courtyard. The first Ducati cruiser was a genuine spaghetti Midwestern, a Yankee-style low rider with a scooped seat, steerhorn handlebar, and chromed bits hither and yon. The Japanese had decided to contest Harley-Davidson's domination of the cruiser market, which apparently encouraged Cagiva to follow suit. Had they but resisted the temptation. . . .

The first Indiana derived from the 650 Alazzurra, though it employed the reversed rear cylinder head. Two 36-mm Bing carburetors rode amidships and the cams were profiled for more urge in the midrange. With its leading-axle Marzocchi fork kicked out at 40 degrees, baloney-slice mufflers, and stepped seat with a sissy bar, the Indiana looked like a country boy gone Vegas. Not only did the machine have the effect of caricature, it was also uncomfortable. Despite its oddities, the Indiana was arguably better as a *motorcycle* than its Japanese counterparts, but resoundingly unsuccessful as a cruiser. Neither Japan nor Italy would pose any serious threat to Milwaukee's control of American-style motorcycle design. Yet.

The rogue Elefant did not suffer any Indiana identity crisis, but it was also up against formidable competitors

from BMW and the Japanese. Introduced in the fall of 1983 and scheduled to be a 750, the Elefant didn't appear in the States in any numbers until 1986, and then only as a 650. But as the terms between Ducati and Cagiva were formalized, the product began to flow, with Cagiva identified on the tank and Ducati on the engine. In 1987 the Elefant did grow to 750-cc, and became a fuel-injected 900 in 1990. Designated the E-900 in the States, the big-bore brush blaster wore the Ducati logo on the tank

By any other name, this was the first Duck that would seriously take to water, sand, dirt, rocks, and all manner of moderately rugged terrain. Not since the 450 R/T had Ducati powered a serious off-road warrior, and Cagiva was eager to expand its competition image beyond Ducati's traditional cafe-racer framework. Cagiva hired former Paris-Dakar winner (1981/1983) Hubert

Auriol away from BMW, but the Bavarians countered with former world motocross champion Gaston Rahier of Belgium, who put the BMW first in the rally in 1984 and 1985. Auriol had been leading in 1985 when he crashed in the final stage of the race.

By 1987, with the acquisition of Husqvarna, Cagiva had compiled a roster of 23 models in the States. The Elefant was offered in a limited edition with Paris-Dakar livery, and the Alazzurra gained a Super Sport version with full fairing and wider cast wheels. Both wore the Cagiva logo, while the Paso, F1, and Indiana retained the Ducati imprint.

The factory hot rod, now designated the F1-B, was in its final iteration as the double overhead-cam four-valve head was reaching maturity. The B model wore an adjustable 40-mm Ceriani fork with a then-trendy anti-dive system. The engine, with slightly hotter cams than

The Bimota DB2 was, as one might expect, the second desmo twin-engined special from Rimini. This exquisite little hummer was built around the Paso 904 engine with a Pantah-style tubular frame rather than the twin-spar aluminum chassis. It was under 400 pounds and over $18,000.
Guy Webster

the previous edition, also had larger valves and a stronger transmission. Unfortunately the F1-B was too loud to meet U.S. noise regulations and couldn't be registered for highway use as imported. Plus it carried a $7,200 price tag in 1987.

The F1S, appearing in 1988, was certifiable everywhere but California, owing to the state's stricter emission controls. For the rest of the country, leaner jetting and Alazzurra mufflers satisfied the federals. The price on this street-legal racer, with passenger seat, was $7,500.

Massimos to the Rescue

The connection between Ducati and Bimota was tenuous from the outset. The db1 was designed by Frederico Martini, formerly of Ducati. Any similarity to the Ducati Paso, designed by Massimo Tamburini, lately of Bimota and now with Cagiva, was entirely feasible. Bimota had been commissioned by Cagiva to build a Pantah-based special; Tamburini had left Bimota to work with Roberto Gallina's Suzuki Grand Prix team. When Tamburini was hired by Cagiva, he drew upon his Bimota experience in designing the Paso. But similarities in the

bodywork notwithstanding, the db1 was much closer to a race replica under the skin; a tightly triangulated frame of straight thin-wall chrome-moly tubing, just over 13 pounds, suspended the 750 twin. With a solo saddle, it weighed under 400 pounds ready to rip, at a cost of $13,000 in the United States.

Bimota had been building cafe customs around Japanese fours for a number of years, and the opportunity to use an Italian engine was welcomed with enthusiasm. The boys in Rimini lavished some care on the project, and the db1 was abundant with nicely fabricated bits and pieces of hardware throughout, and the chassis/engine interface was tidy and compact. Like any well-engineered, athletic young Italian, gender optional, the db1 looked just as good with its clothes off as on.

By this time, four-stroke "production" racing for twins had taken different paths in Europe and the United States. Both divisions were built on the 1,000-cc twin vs. 750-cc four formula, but Europe's TT Formula One allowed special racing frames. Stateside Superbike, primarily to minimize the cost for privateers, specified production frames. The American model would prevail, and Ducati was prepared for the future with an eight-valve 850-cc twin, which it presented at Daytona in 1987. Relegated to the Pro Twins class, since it was not yet a production model, the desmoquattro made 120 rear-wheel horsepower and clipped the traps at 165 miles per hour. In the hands of Marco Lucchinelli, the Ducati top-dogged the privateer twins with a speed that would have been good for eighth place in the Superbike race. Lucky had won the 1986 Battle of the Twins on the F1.

Superbike racing had ripened since the powered-up but ill-handling Japanese fours appeared at Daytona in 1975. As racer John Long said, "The rear end chatters under braking, and they don't know if they can turn or not, so they have to go straight until they feel safe." The fours handled smartly by 1988, so Ducati had to make more power, which would create new issues with the chassis, suspension, riding styles, and so forth. The Castiglionis knew that Ducati would have to reclaim its honor on the racetrack in order to keep pace in the leap-frogging sportbike market.

Thus did Massimo Bordi's 1975 engineering thesis come to life; now as a liquid- rather than air-cooled double overhead-cam desmo twin, valves disposed at 40 degrees, Ferrari-style Weber-Marelli computerized ignition/injection system, and close-ratio six-speed transmission. The first versions in 1988, fitted with headlight and electric-start but not yet street-legal, carried a $21,000 price tag. The original 851 chassis boasted 57 inches of wheelbase, a 24-degree steering head, and 16-inch wheels with 4.7 inches of travel at each end.

Ducati, for the first time in quite a few years, now had the money to develop a new racing motorcycle. Fabio Taglioni was still involved in the process, mostly out of respect for the good Doctor's past contributions, but this was Bordi's baby. "I came here in 1978 and became technical director in 1982," says Massimo Bordi today, "so everything we did from 1982 up to now depended only on my decisions." His first four years were split between the final bevel-drive twins and the Pantah. "But the first big project was in '86, when I decided to put into production the original idea of my thesis, four-valve desmo. I had some talk with Taglioni, and the point was that he did not trust the four-valve, because he did some testing in 1976 on the bevel-drive and did not get good results.

"He wanted to build a four-cylinder two-valve," Bordi continues, "and I was insisting we make a 90-degree twin four-valve, to be different from the Japanese, to respect our heritage and go on with our strategy."

The key to making that work, Bordi said, was using a chamber design similar to that of the Cosworth engine, with one spark plug in the middle of four valve heads with a very straight inlet manifold. The results speak for themselves.

Former motocrosser Giancarlo Falappa joined Frenchman Raymond Roche on the Ducati team in 1990 and won at Donnington Park in Britain. Crashes in Canada and Austria put the popular Italian out of contention, and he was replaced late in the season by American rider Jamie James.

This photograph hangs behind Massimo Bordi's desk in Bologna. The subject of his engineering thesis materialized with Cosworth-style four-valve heads, Ferrari-style computerized fuel injection, and desmo valves. Modified Pantah crankcases went into the space frame derived from the TT1.

for the Ferrari F40. Efforts to solve the engine's breathing problems pushed the displacement to 851-cc and a 25-horsepower increase. The added power brought new difficulties dialing in the fuel injection, and introduced reliability questions about rods and pistons. By 1988 the engine and chassis were sorted out, just in time for the inauguration of the World Superbike Championship and some interesting contests in the United States.

One of the factory bikes, ridden by Stefano Caracchi, was second in ProTwins at Daytona in 1988. The 851 was then inherited by Eraldo Ferracci, proprietor of Fast By Ferracci of Pennsylvania, and with rider Dale Quarterly aboard went on to win the ProTwins Championship. Ferracci fiddled and finessed the eight-valve, knocked off about 40 pounds, and improved the weight distribution. He also reworked the heads and the exhaust system, and the motorcycle was indeed wickedly fast. Ferracci also had one advantage on the field—direct access to the latest ROM chips from Italy. The arrival of mapped fuel injection was the result of Ducati's relationship of mutual respect with Ferrari, which used the Weber system in Formula One racing.

To the average sport rider, the 851 at $21,000 was about as affordable as a Ferrari. The civilian model, the street-legal 851 Sport, was rather more attainable at

The 1987 851 Strada prototype had Paso-style turn signal/mirror pods on the fairing. Ducati built 200 851 Superbikes and 300 of the Stradas to meet the Superbike rules for homologation. The first production Strada would retain the 16-inch Marvic composite wheels.

In 1986 the prototype for the *desmoquattro* was a 748-cc racer entrusted to Virginio Ferrari, Marco Lucchinelli, and Juan Garriga of Spain. Bordi, Farné, and associates put the project together in less than nine months, employing the Weber fuel injection developed

The first batch of 851 Superbikes were fitted with the race-replica's braced swingarm, 17-inch Marvic magnesium wheels, Marzocchi MR1 fork, and racing exhaust system. The factory kit gave the Superbike a 20-horsepower edge on the Strada, and the price was only about 20 percent higher. Guy Webster

$10,900. And for the Ducatisti on a tighter budget, Bologna offered the 750 Sport, the next devolutionary edition of the F1, at $6,700.

The 851 Superbike Strada, the first desmoquattro road model, came on the market in 1988. Few of the red, white, and green machines came to the United States in street trim, and most of the first Stateside 851s were the expensive racing models. For 1989 the tri-color scheme was supplanted by red bodywork and white 17-inch wheels, and the mirrors were moved to stalks mounted higher on the fairing.

At 500 pounds on the road, with almost 80 horsepower at the rear wheel, the 851 was hardly a race replica; but it was a 150-miles-per-hour machine that ran the quarter-mile in the low 11s. Not so shabby for a V-twin, and a certain signal that Ducati would once again be taken quite seriously, especially in Japan. It was also a hopeful sign that, barring papal intervention or a complete economic collapse in Italy, the venerable V-twins would keep stride in the 1990s. That they would come to lead the pack was something of a surprise to most veteran observers, even the optimists among them, and once again, most notably in Japan.

Synthesizing the Superbikes

Part two of Ducati's renaissance focused on the air-cooled two-valve desmo, in Economy, Supersport, and GT trim. The 750 Sport was entered in the budget division, the Paso/907 filled the GT description, and the forthcoming 900 SS would be the Supersport for the masses. Work would meanwhile continue on the next iteration of the Superbike engine, the 888.

The 750 Sport had little in common with its forebear of 1973, though they were roughly equal in terms of power, weight, and top speed. Both were powered by air-cooled engines with carburetors, but the new Sport carried a single carb situated between the cylinders. The Weber mixer, in concert with a restrictive exhaust system, created the same stumble-down staggers experienced by Paso riders. And while its Japanese competitors sported six-speed gearboxes, the F-1 soldiered on with only five. Finally, the bike's trendy 16-inch wheels spoiled the bikes proportions and failed to reduce steering effort significantly. Nonetheless, the 750 sold in substantial numbers in England and led to the creation of a 900. While both models were dismissed as parts-bin specials by the desmodromically hip, both were also capable pavement strafers despite their shortcomings.

Parts-bin parentage notwithstanding, the new Sport carried many of the F1 attributes into wider distribution for under $7,000. This was still an extravagance compared to the cost/benefit ratio of numerous other 750-cc–plus mounts with four cylinders, but it was a piece of Italian handling magic for about $1,000 more than a new Suzuki Katana 1100. For the true believer, no real choice at all.

With lackluster results from the Paso, Cagiva saw some wisdom in refurbishing the F1. So the 750 Sport, sans elephant logo, was released in 1988 and proved the lasting appeal of an air-cooled V-twin. In 1989 the 900 Supersport arrived with an air-cooled version of the Paso 906 engine and six-speed transmission, wide 17-inch wheels, and Brembo four-piston calipers at both ends. The exhaust system derived from the 851, but the problem of clumsy carburetion with the dual-throat Weber remained. Both the 750 Sport and 900 Supersport were interim models, to be superseded in 1991.

Although only about 2,000 each of the 750s and 900s were built, most remain on the road and have escaped collectibility for the time being. While most of the annoyance factors could be corrected, the revivalist Sports were still a bit narrowly defined for the U.S. market. The new Supersport would offer a more comfortable riding position and two Mikuni carburetors.

By 1990 the Cagiva conjugation was fully up to speed. Edi Orioli and the Elefant 900 became the first Italian rider/bike combination to win the Paris-Dakar rally, and the 888, the first derivation of the 851, was the

Dale Quarterly and Eraldo Ferracci teamed up to display the 851 Superbike's capabilities on American racetracks. Ferracci's connections with the Ducati factory enabled him to get the newest trick bits quickly, and Quarterly went on to win the AMA ProTwins championship in 1988. Tom Riles

model that would put Ducati at the head of the Superbike class. ProTwins had become something of a semi-factory GP class in the States, although most of the major players still qualified as privateers. But not many self-funded racers could afford $35,000 for a factory Ducati 888.

At Daytona in 1990, Louisiana's Jamie James qualified the Fast By Ferracci Ducati on the front row. Unfortunately a first-turn accident put him out of the race; James had previously won the ProTwins event. World Superbike racing, inaugurated in 1988, had now matured in terms of both equipment and riders. The formula provided twins with both weight and displacement advantages in order to equalize performance with the four-cylinder bikes. The 750-cc fours had a minimum weight of 363.3 pounds, while the 1,000-cc twins could weigh as little as 330 pounds. Honda had clearly seen the marketing potential offered by Superbike racing and built the compact RC30 V-4, with gear-driven cams and a redline close to 14,000 rpm. American Fred Merkel had won the 1988 and 1989 World Superbike titles aboard the tidy—and tiny—Honda.

By 1990 the Ducati, still well shy of the 1,000-cc limit for twins, was already on the performance plane with the RC30 and the Yamaha OW 01 fours, and grumbling about the twins' weight and displacement premiums began early. The nattering was put on hold at

The new 900 Super Sport didn't match the heritage of its model name either, and was powered by the 904-cc Paso engine but without liquid cooling. The Weber carburetor remained, but the 900 got the 17-inch wheels, better brakes, and suspension from the previous 851.

The 750 Sport of 1989–1990 was a hybrid model with the air/oil-cooled Paso engine in a modified F1 frame. The Weber carburetor, 16-inch wheels, and nonadjustable suspension did little to elevate the 750 Sport to the heights of its 1970s namesake, but the low price appealed to some first-time Ducati buyers. Bill McMillan

By 1990, Eraldo Ferracci was established as the U.S. Ducati wizard in residence. Jamie James became the overdog of the ProTwins class, won handily at Daytona, and also qualified on the pole for the Superbike event. James later logged two second-place finishes at Mosport. Tom Riles

Raymond Roche came second to Fred Merkel's Honda in the 1989 World Superbike Championship, and won the title in 1990. Ducati had now found the proper combination of useful horsepower, handling, and reliability to finish well consistently. Staying on top would renew the challenge.

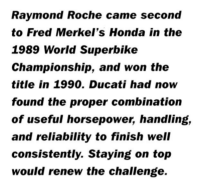

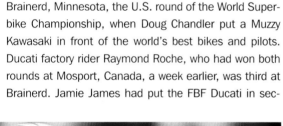

Brainerd, Minnesota, the U.S. round of the World Superbike Championship, when Doug Chandler put a Muzzy Kawasaki in front of the world's best bikes and pilots. Ducati factory rider Raymond Roche, who had won both rounds at Mosport, Canada, a week earlier, was third at Brainerd. Jamie James had put the FBF Ducati in sec-

ond place in both Mosport races. Frenchman Roche went on to win the World Superbike Championship in 1990, with the factory effort managed by Marco Lucchinelli, and Ducati would show little inclination to surrender this position for the rest of the decade.

In 1990 the 851, nee 888, was available in the United States, at $19,500 in quite limited numbers. A fully adjustable Ohlins inverted fork and gas shock replaced the previous Marzocchi suspenders. Rear ride height could be set independently, and the steering head angle was set a half-degree shorter than the 851's. Aluminum cam-belt pulleys replaced the steel items, and the cams had considerably more lift and duration. The 851 employed 29 degrees of valve overlap, while the 888 was set at 86 degrees, the interlude fed by an additional injector in each 50-mm throttle body. The 888 SP (Sport Production) made 96 horsepower at 9,000 rpm, weighed 450 pounds, and went 152 miles per hour.

The 888 carried Roche to eight wins in his championship effort for 1990 and was steadily refined throughout the season. Carbon fiber mufflers, tail section, and front fender, as well as a smaller radiator, reduced overall weight by more than 20 pounds. A limited number of Roche Replicas were built, employing the inverted Ohlins fork and Marvic magnesium wheels. The street-legal 851 SP2 now had many of the same top-shelf compo-

nents and was good for close to 160 miles per hour, while the heavier and considerably less expensive Strada topped out at 150.

In little more than 10 years, Cagiva had brought Ducati from near collapse to prosperity and championship status in international roadracing. The Castiglionis had restored Husqvarna to health as well, and finally achieved victory with the Elefant in the daunting Paris-Dakar competition. They also had developed and refined the 500-cc, four-cylinder, two-stroke Grand Prix machine to compete with the powerful Japanese factory teams.

The brothers' enthusiasm for racing was intrumental in establishing the creditable Cagiva imprint worldwide, and responsible in large measure for Ducati's thundering success in Superbike racing. Of course none of these achievements had come cheaply, and the old process of robbing Pietro to pay Paolo would limit Cagiva's glory days to a period of about five years. But

within this time frame the lads from Varese managed to make a lasting impression.

Even as the Castiglionis were spending themselves into a corner, Ducati's desmo renaissance was in full bloom. Bologna was building more models and selling them in greater numbers than ever before. The brothers had been able to upgrade production facilities, hire more engineers, and adopt some computer-based systems in manufacturing and testing. Ducati had done its part by refining the Pantah-based models into reliable and affordable sporting machines for the road, and also cultivating and massaging the same power plant into a Cosworth-style racing motor capable of beating the best Japanese production racers. Quite some achievement, most informed observers agreed, but how long could such a state of affairs last? Much longer, as it turned out, than nearly anyone might have predicted in 1991.

Just as the Leoni/Adamo connection had served Ducati well in the lean years, the Fast By Ferracci team provided Bologna with an advanced-guard R&D department in the States. Dale Quarterly and Jamie James advanced the cause, and with Doug Polen, Ferracci would conquer the world. Tom Riles

CHAPTER 6

World Champs, Monsters, & Yankee Dollars

1991-2001

Ducati had powered into the 1990s as motorcyling's most successful anachronism, next to Harley-Davidson. But the booming Bolognese twins had toppled formidable opponents on the track before, and subsequent success with road models hadn't followed. How long could the "old technology" prevail? This question would be answered, first by Bordi, then with supporting evidence from Eraldo Ferracci, Doug Polen, and Carl Fogarty. And then by the friendly Monsters, the 916 and the money men from America.

The question, it seems, had been improperly framed. For the technology was not old, but was in fact informed by contemporary engineering and racing results. The basic design was certainly mature, but the materials, computerized tools, testing, and spirit of creative inquiry were state of the art. The first example was the redesigned 900 SS, the new user-friendly Italian roadster. It was easy to ride fast, but not too painful for occasional duty around town. By fitting the Paso 906 engine, sans liquid-cooling, Ducati had fashioned a reasonably fast and affordable sportster without incurring crippling expenditures for new tooling or parts.

The new 900 SS marked a notable elevation in componentry and integrated packaging. The Showa suspension, complemented by Brembo Gold Line four-piston calipers and 320-mm front

Ducati's desmoquattro Superbikes, shown here in 996 form, reinvigorated Ducati in the 1990s. Tod Rafferty

The history of Ducati's racing ascendance in the 1990s stands displayed in Bologna's Ducati Museo.

rotors, offered broadly adjustable handling and linear deceleration. The air/oil–cooled engine had the benefit of stronger cases and two additional clutch plates from the 851 S. Throttle response was improved considerably by the 38-mm Mikuni carburetors with equal-length intake tracts, and handling benefited from 2 degrees of tuck in the steering head and and a shortened aluminum swingarm that gave 55.5 inches of wheelbase. The 41-mm inverted Showa fork and slightly longer shock absorber added another measure of poise, and the riding position had been relaxed by elevating the handlebars and lowering the footpegs. The 900 SS was offered with a full or half fairing, and was quickly recognized as the best combination of high-speed agility and everyday civility to ever roll out of Bologna.

While the 900 SS may have lacked some of the eclectic charm and engineering panache of its bevel-drive ancestor of the 1960s, it was happier and far less troublesome in the real world. In its road test, Cycle magazine declared the 900 SS "simply the best street bike Ducati has ever built." The high praise was partially the result of the new European Common Market, which had relaxed trade barriers and allowed Ducati to buy some of its important components outside Italy for the first time. With the advent of Mikuni carburetors and Showa suspension, Ducati had adjusted upward the level of user-friendliness, and the hinged fuel tank afforded easy access to the battery and airbox.

Detractors could argue, not without reason, that the 900 SS was merely another example of Ducati's traditional parts-bin provenance. On the other hand, it was also "the fastest street-legal twin Cycle has ever tested, and not far off the standards set by the Japanese 750 fours." New aluminum bolt-on hangers for the pegs and mufflers were tasteful touches, and the overall styling was more open, notably on the half-faired version, although the oil cooler looked vulnerable hanging from the front cylinder head and cluttered up the engine. And while the chatterbox dry clutch, aggravated by a high overall gear ratio, could be annoying, the 900 SS quickly became a Bolognese benchmark.

The Paso 907 IE, now at the end of its run, sold for $8,800 and the 851 Superbike went for $12,000. So the 900 SS, at just under $8,000, was only $700 more than the outstanding Honda VFR 750, and about 50 pounds lighter. The 851 was still $3,000–5,000 more than its Japanese street Superbike counterparts, and the racing version was available for about $25,000.

In 1992 the cast-iron valve guides in the 900 SS were replaced by aluminum-bronze pieces, a stronger clutch was fitted, and black paint was added as an optional color. Production numbers matched the previous year. The 900 was then joined by a new iteration of the 750 SS, configured as an entry-level sporty rather than a revival of its 1970s namesake. With Pantah crankcases, the non-adjustable Showa fork, and a single front disc brake, the 750 SS was priced $1,000 below the 900. The 750 employed the same 38-mm flat-slide Mikuni carburetors, which were jetted lean to meet U.S. emissions regulations and caused a surge at idle and a flat spot in the midrange. The Pantah wet clutch, while quieter than the dry system on the 900, was hobbled by stiff lever action despite its hydraulic actuation. But at just over $7,000, and carrying 25 pounds less than the 900, the 750 SS eased the entry requirements to the brotherhood of racy red roadsters from Bologna.

Also introduced in 1992, the limited edition 900 Superlight featured Marvic composite wheels, high pipes, solo seat, and a carbon fiber front fender. Although it came in only 15 pounds under the standard 900 SS, the Superlight was also distinguished by a production number plate on the triple clamp. Its exclusivity was diminished, however, when the original run of 500 grew to more than 1,300 of the 1992 models.

907 IE Arrivederci

The streamlined 907 IE, formerly the Paso, was now accorded some of the accoutrements of its sportier brethren. The *iniezione eletronica* was the Weber-Marelli system from the 851, using smaller throttle bodies; and the lumpier cams were imported from the previous 900 SS. The stronger crankcases also made it to the last of the Pasos, and the engine was good for nearly 10 more horsepower than the previous 906. It possessed sufficient urge for under 12-second quarter-mile times and a top speed of 136 miles per hour, not so shabby for a 500-pound twin.

The 907 chassis was also revised with the adoption of the 851's stout swingarm, and slightly longer Marzocchi M1R fork. These components, and the new 17-inch wheels, brought the wheelbase to 58.5 inches and gave 4.2 inches of trail. With the steering head angle at 25 degrees, the 907 handled better than its overall dimensions might indicate. While the Tamburini-designed streamliner did not derive from the race-bred lineage of Ducati twins, and was configured for touring comfort, the 907 was no slouch on the back roads. With suspension at both ends adjustable for both compression and rebound damping, and good weight distribution, the most post-haste of the Pasos could run with much sportier mounts in the twisties.

But with a price of $8,800, and exceptional competitors like the Honda VFR 750 selling for $7,000, the 907 was on its way to early retirement. New and larger Brembo front brakes were fitted in 1992, and metallic black offered as an optional color. But this would be the last model year, and another full-enclosure motorcycle

Not until mid-1991 did the truly new 900 Supersport (now one word) arrive Stateside in any numbers. Although based on the 1990 version, the new SS was sufficiently redrawn to qualify as a new model. Well received by press and populace worldwide, the 900 SS would have a seven-year run.
Nick Cedar

passed quietly into history. Designer Massimo Tamburini would go on to create the Ducati 916, which would be developed concurrently (read *slowly*) with the Cagiva 500-cc two-stroke GP racer. The Bimota cofounder's most recent creation is the new MV Agusta F4.

851 Superbike

For hard-nosed sport riders who found the 900 SS too civilized, and could afford the added $4,000 pre-mium, Ducati offered the 851 S. The extra bucks bought a liquid-cooled engine with Weber-Marelli fuel injection, double overhead cams, and four valves per cylinder. The 851, now in its fifth year of production, had been steadily upgraded in the traditional Italian fashion of incremental improvement. The dual seat was adopted on the Strada in 1990, requiring a heavier rear subframe, and the expensive Austrian Pankl connecting rods were replaced by standard Pantah units. In 1991 the road model arrived with the Showa inverted front fork and an Ohlins shock absorber. Even with a slightly lower compression ratio and more weight, the 851 was still arguably the reigning king of cafe racer cachet. But the nearly $9,000 price tag, almost twice the price of the Suzuki GSXR 750, put serious constraints on its success.

Now that the more socialized 900 SS was on line, Ducati brought more focus to bear on the racing versions of the 851. Bologna had nonetheless remained steadfast, despite the new corporate emphasis on road models, in their long tradition of building race replicas for both privateer racers and road riders. In 1992 the 851 Superbike roadster used the larger valves from the 888, compression was 11:1, and the electronic fuel injection mapping was revised, which produced a 6-horsepower increase.

A new curved radiator allowed tighter bodywork and effected better aerodynamics. The Superbike made 91 rear-wheel horsepower and topped out at 147 miles per hour, but the powerful Brembo front brakes were compromised by rubber hydraulic lines that confused feedback at the lever. The price was $12,500.

The 851 SP (Sport Production) retained the same numeric designation even though displacement had been 888-cc for four years. In 1991 the SP3 gained some ground clearance with an upswept exhaust system. With Ohlins suspension, wider wheels, and an aluminum fuel tank, the SP was 50 pounds lighter than the Strada. The Corsa (racing) model; given a carbon fiber tank and tail section it dropped another 65 pounds. Bologna produced 30 Corsas in 1991 and 50 in 1992. The Raymond Roche Replica dispensed with the electric starter, lights, and unnecessary road equipment. Carbon fiber, titanium, and magnesium bits and pieces brought the weight down below 400 pounds, and the price up to $55,000.

In 1992 the 851 label gave way to the more accurate and symmetrical 888 designation, and Ducati introduced the SPS (Sport Production Special), fitted with a carbon fiber tank, tail section, and mufflers. The Special also had slightly larger valves than the SP and revised fuel-injection mapping, which delivered an expanded torque spread and an additional 10 horsepower. The engine was built to Corsa specs, with a stronger clutch and main bearings, and the fanless racing radiator. Only 100 of the lightweight roadsters were produced.

Kenny to Randy to Eddie to Johnny

Cagiva had been chasing victory in Grand Prix racing for eight years, with little success, and decided in 1985 to obtain the services of a world-class rider. Randy

Mamola had suggested they take the bike out to the middle of Lake Como and dump it overboard. Three-time world champion Kenny Roberts, still under contract to Yamaha, tested the bike at Misano and set a new lap record. "I tested for them in '85, with Yamaha's best wishes, because they were lost. It was to everybody's advantage at that time to keep all the factories in there." Cagiva wanted Roberts as lead rider in 1986, and asked him to name his price. "They said we know it's going to be expensive, but how much?" Roberts says. "But I wouldn't say, because I didn't want to do that. They were relentless, but I turned it down. And I think they were a little put out that I wouldn't name a price."

It wasn't that Roberts had reservations about the machine. "It was a serious contender, and it would have been a great challenge for me. But I had a contract with Yamaha, and I didn't want to race anymore. But eventually they got to where they could win a Gran Prix. I said that it handled better than the Yamaha, and Eddie said the same thing. It didn't have the performance it needed, and we helped them with that."

The Castiglionis' holy mission was to re-create the legend of MV Agusta, to recapture the heady era of Surtees, Hailwood, Agostini, and Redman. The MV marque was not on the auction block, so Cagiva had to settle for painting the Yamaha-derived 500-cc two-stroke fours in the traditional red and silver livery of the Meccanica Verghera racers. After more than a decade without satisfactory results, Cagiva announced their GP retirement in

1990. Instead, for 1991 they signed Eddie Lawson, four-time world champion, to develop the motorcycle, built a new racing shop in Varese, and hired several new engineers. Lawson did post their first GP victory at the Hungarian round in 1992, but could only manage ninth place in the season standings. With Lawson's retirement in 1993, Cagiva hired John Kocinski, who had placed third on the Roberts Marlboro Yamaha in 1992, and Doug Chandler, who had been fifth on the Lucky Strike Suzuki.

Paddock scuttlebutt posited that one of Cagiva's problems was an increasingly adversarial relationship between Lawson and Giacomo Agostini. "That goes back a few years, to the Marlboro days," Roberts says. "In my opinion, and I'm just an outsider, I don't think Ago treated Eddie very well. Which is not a surprise, because Ago didn't treat anybody very well. I never had a problem with Ago when I raced for him, but Eddie certainly did. And I would have to say that some of it was not Agostini's fault; the motorcycles were falling further behind."

Polen to Fogarty to Fame

In the early 1990s, two young men emerged from the racing ranks to post the Ducati colors on international

The bike Raymond Roche rode to the 1990 World Superbike Championship now sits in the Ducati Museum. Thirty examples of the Roche Replica were built in 1990, and another 50 in 1991, with most of the racer's goodies. The price was $50,000-plus, with spares. George Fogarty bought one. Tod Rafferty

Eddie Lawson, having won four 500-cc Grand Prix titles, found a good market in Italy for development riders. Unfortunately, Cagiva's 500-cc Grand Prix program saw more valleys than peaks.

podiums with regularity and in convincing fashion. From distinctly different countries, England and Texas, the two riders shared a common economy of style, deliberate focus, and an intense desire to win races. At age 26, Doug Polen of Corinth, Texas, had retired once from road-racing when he entered the American Suzuki Cup Series in 1986. As a dominant club racer, Polen soon became the first journeyman pivateer roadracer in the country to make decent money in the sport. He found this agree-able, and soon enough his abilities had attracted offers of sponsorship. When Eraldo Ferracci asked Polen to ride for his Ducati team in 1991, the offer was accepted.

In England, the Fogartys of Blackburn, Lancashire, had been a racing family for some decades. George came second in the Schweppes Jubilee 1,000-cc class at the Isle of Man in 1977, riding a Suzuki 750. He then rode the NCR/Sport Cycles' Ducati twins and did well in the 600-cc TT2 division. His son Carl showed an affinity for the sport and a willingness to watch and listen to his daddy, and fellow riders like Mike Hailwood and Joey Dunlop. Young Fogarty won the the world Formula One title three years running, and set a new lap record at the Isle of Man in 1992, running a 123.6-miles per hour loop on a Yamaha OW01. The same year he put a Yamaha up with the front-runners at the British 500-cc Grand Prix at Donnington Park, and grabbed consider-able attention. Earlier in the season, Fogarty had posted his Ducati credentials with a World Superbike win on the same track, and later signed to ride for the factory the following year, when he would be 26.

"I had actually quit racing in 1983," Doug Polen said. "I just got tired of racing for two-dollar trophies; there was no way to make any money at it. Then I came back in '86 to ride the Suzuki Cup Series. That was the first time I could afford to get to some of the better tracks around the country." After riding for the Yoshimura Suzuki team, Polen teamed up with Eraldo Ferracci for World Superbike in 1991, and the combination was all but invincible. The Texan won 17 of the 24 races to grab the championship. "I was basically the only guy on a competitive bike," Polen recalls, "because of the Dunlop tires. Things got much tougher in 1992."

Polen had established himself solidly as the preemi-nent rider in the division and helped solidify Ferracci's relationship with Bologna. Eraldo had a long-standing agreement with Massimo Bordi, which provided him access to the latest racing improvements from the factory, but Ferracci financed most of the racing program from his

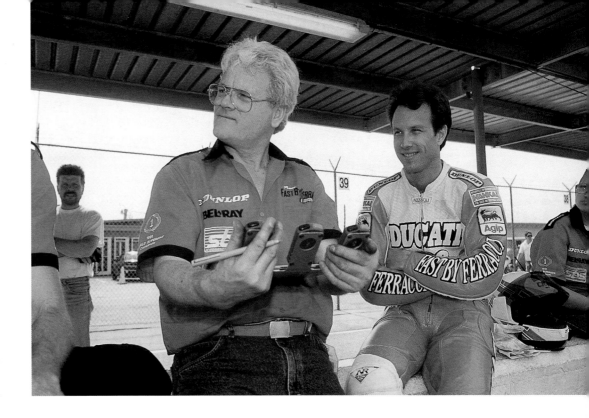

own parts and service company, Fast By Ferracci. This arrangement allowed Ferracci to avoid any dependence on the management at Cagiva North America, who were far more interested in selling motorcycles than in racing them, and saw no tangible connection between the two.

The other Italian-American arm of Ducati Racing was Gio.Ca.Moto, a performance parts business created by former NCR mechanic and Ducati manager Giorgio Casolari. GCM had grown from a Ducati racing and repair shop to a major aftermarket supplier, and in 1985 Casolari teamed up with Reno Leoni and Jimmy Adamo to establish a U.S. distributorship. So Ducati effectively had two Italian-American satellite R&D departments, with information, assistance, and parts flowing both ways between the United States and Italy. Casolari had considerable experience with specialized parts for endurance racing, and Ferracci had become expert at tuning and setting up machines for American circuits. In 1998, Ducati purhased Gio.Ca.Moto and joined it with Ducati Performance, now headed by Daniele Casolari.

Polen was drafted to join Raymond Roche and Giancarlo Falappa on the factory team in 1992, though he remained under the Ferracci banner. The level of the game in Superbike racing was rising sharply, and the stakes with them. Rumors of friction between old and new team members circulated, as they do every sea-son, especially in multinational teams. "I wouldn't say

Eraldo Ferracci (left) and Doug Polen became The Team in 1991, and the former club racer from Texas gained international notice. Team Fast By Ferracci, Ducati Corse USA, dominated the World Superbike series as the Lone Star Streak won 17 of the 23 championship rounds. Tom Riles

Number 23 appeared prominently and often in the motopress. Polen's abilities, Ferracci's tuning techniques, and Dunlop radial tires proved the perfect competition package in 1991. The Ducati vanguard also included 1990 champ Raymond Roche, Giancarlo Falappa, and Stephane Mertens. Tom Riles

there was any real friction," Polen says now. "There's always going to be some tension among teammates, whether or not they are different nationalities." Only 16 points separated Polen and Roche with two races remaining in the 1992 season. Was there a European conspiracy to block the American's chances and aid the Frenchman? "I don't know if there was any plan," said Polen, "but there was some suspect riding at that last race in New Zealand that year. I wouldn't want to say any more than that, but it was suspect." Polen won the first race, came second in the final go, and won the title by 35 points over Roche, with Australian Rob Phillis' Kawasaki in third.

Doug Polen's goal was to win both the World and American Superbike titles in 1992, which he may well

have accomplished had several U.S. dates not conflicted with European rounds. As it was he finished third in the States and conducted some epic tussles with Kawasaki's Scott Russell in the process. At Brainerd, Minnesota, the Texas twister had a 23-second margin on Jamie James' Yamaha at the flag, in a 60-mile race. In 1993, Russell and Polen swapped positions, the Georgian winning the World Superbike title for Kawasaki and the FBF Ducati pilot taking the American title. Ducati had hoped to do the double that year, with Polen in the AMA series and Carl Fogarty in the World events. Russell, who had also been offered a lucrative contract to ride for Ducati, chose to stay with Muzzy. Kawasaki and a three-year deal. Fogarty finished the 1994 series in second place.

The Boy of George

On his way to becoming king, Carl Fogarty gathered a growing throng of enthusiastic fans in his homeland. "Carl's first-ever race was on my Formula Two 600 Ducati," George Fogarty said, "which I loaned him for the last three months of the year in 1983. In 1984 he went on to ride the 250 Yamaha, broke the lap record at Silverstone and won the race. It's always been the same, wherever he's been. In '88 and '89 Carl rode my Honda in the world Formula One championship, and he won it in '88, '89, and '90.

"In '92 I had just sold my company, a transport and warehouse business. So I went down and bought a top-of-the-range road Ducati, a transporter, and we took a mechanic on to do the World Superbike Championships. We also joined Kawasaki France to do the World Endurance Championship, and Carl rode for Yamaha in the TT. [On the unfamiliar OW01, Fogarty had a 40-second lead at 180 of 226 miles when the gearbox broke.]

"It came to the second round of the World Superbike at Donnington Park, and Carl is on an over-the-counter, road-going Ducati. He qualified on the pole position; he knocked 1 second off Doug Polen's previous lap record. He was faster than all the works machines. After about 18 laps Carl was 7 seconds in front of everyone, then he slides off. I came back to the paddock, from watchin' half-way 'round the circuit, and I thought he was trying too hard. I shouted at him and told him off, to have such a big lead and then fall off. He started crying. And they all said George, he wasn't trying too hard, he just took a different line. There was oil on the track and he had to take a tighter line, and he just went.

"In the second race, on the first lap he was 12th, and every single lap he passed a rider until he finally passed Scott Russell to take the lead, and won it. That was on a top-of-the-range road bike; it just goes to show you what a brilliant rider can do, just on sheer ability. At the end of that season I got two phone calls from Ducati people, asking if they could have Carl for the following year, and that was it. Best thing that ever happened to me and to him, because up to then I'd been funding it all myself, for that year. That's why we rode for Loctite Yamaha at the TT, where Carl's lap record from '92 still stands today; then he rode in the World Endurance Championships for Kawasaki France and he won that."

While Carl Fogarty's $50,000-plus (with spares) Ducati Corsa may stretch the definition of a road bike, it certainly was top-shelf hardware, and the young Briton did

go out and spank the factory riders at Donnington. "He can ride any type of bike anywhere, can that lad," declares a proud poppa George. "When he's in a race, in the right frame of mind, no one in the world can stop him."

Monster Hits

Miguel Galluzzi's design for the Ducati Monster effectively created today's sport-cruiser category. Until *Il Mostro*, no one else had noticed a hole in the market, but the basic sport cruiser filled a demographic spectrum overlooked for years. Yamaha had owned the muscle-bound-cruiser segment with the V-Max for nearly a decade, and all the Japanese builders offered low-rider and touring-style limo-bikes patterned on the Harley-Davidson profile. Japan also put forward various standard or naked models, fashioned in the style of their production models of the 1970s and 1980s. The Monster, though, harkened back to an earlier era.

American riders of the 1940s and 1950s called them bobbers, trackers, or alley racers, standard models trimmed for style, fun, and the absence of extraneous bits and pieces. And weight. These were most often Indians or Harleys in the States, and eventually Norton, Triumph, and BSA joined the parade. Cagiva's first cruiser, the Indiana, was an unintentional caricature of

Polen stalking Colin Edwards and Yvon DuHamel at Daytona; the draftsman's paradise. In 1992, Polen won his second World Superbike Championship, with Raymond Roche again in second place. The 888 was now down to 330 pounds, and gathered 135 horsepower at the rear wheel. Tom Riles

met with overwhelming support among the management, but he was persistent, and the decision eventually came down for a limited production of 1,000 machines. Following the Monster's debut at the Cologne show in 1992, and the rapturous response of press and public, the build number was bumped to 5,000. Few Cagivans (and probably no Ducatisti) could have recognized the brilliance of the Monster concept at the time. The brawny boulevardier was at once stylish, easy and fun to ride, relatively affordable, and a good all-round performer. It was also the perfect platform for all manner of optional accessories and inventive aftermarket parts and decorations.

The engine was imported directly from the 900 SS without modification. The Monster's front frame section came from the 888, attached to new rear bracketry to accommodate the sloping tank and seat. The 904-cc engine and 41-mm inverted Showa fork were standard Supersport; the wheels (5.5-inch rear, 3.5-inch front) and fat 17-inch radial tires applied generous traction, enhanced by an adjustable linkage-control rear Boge shock absorber. The steering head sat at 24 degrees, with 4 inches of trail and a 56.3-inch wheelbase; at 435 pounds the street scratcher weighed in with the Sports of 20 years earlier. Acceleration, speed, and handling

In 1993, Ferracci and Polen stayed home and won the AMA National Superbike series. Carl Fogarty and Giancarlo Falappa composed Ducati's World Superbike team, managed by Raymond Roche. The support team, under Davide Tardozzi, was manned by Stephane Mertens and Juan Garriga. Tom Riles

the American style of the 1970s, when the chopper revival was in vogue. The Monster, however, was a genuine bad boy from an altogether different stable, and but for the tank and seat, it derived from existing parts.

Designer Galluzzi had worked for Honda's European design facility before moving to Cagiva in 1990. His notions for a variation on the Ducati style were not

Ducati hoped for World and U.S. Superbike titles, but Scott Russell and Kawasaki grabbed the WSB title. Polen, shown here in the winner's circle with Colin Edwards (left) and Dale Quarterly, upheld his end by winning the American championship. Polen would switch to Honda in 1994. Tom Riles

were all superior to its predecessors', and the bobber styling reduced the intimidation factor for novice riders. The Monster was a friendly tough guy, the Popeye of moto-brawlers.

And the M900, officially named, was eminently roadworthy, on top of its winning appearance, its brio, machismo, and fundamental simplicity—what the French call its *bon temps roulez (let the good times roll)*. With the Monster, Cagiva had expanded the Ducati market profile without diluting it. The recognition that not all fans of Italian style and performance needed or wanted a street-legal roadracer came to serve Ducati well, in the face of yet another impending reorganization of its management. Monsters made money.

Supermono Pompone

Taglioni had been inspired by the prospect of transforming his desmo single into a 90-degree V-twin. With the passage of two decades, his successor, Massimo Bordi, was intrigued by the opposite proposition, redesigning the twin as a single. The Supermono utilized the 851 twin crankcases, with the real cylinder down in front and a dummy piston on top for balance. Bordi was out to build a short-stroke, high-rpm single that made serious power and little vibration, and was not inclined to add the complexity of balance shafts. While the dummy piston effectively canceled both primary and secondary imbalances, it also absorbed useful horsepower. Bordi's final design eliminated the prosthetic piston and cylinder, replacing it with a lever at right angles to the secondary connecting rod and pivoted at the other end on a pin at the front of the crankcase. A bulge cast into the cases covered the balance system.

The new solution dispensed with high frictional losses and crankcase pressure pulses and pushed horsepower from 53 to 63 at 10,500 rpm. A healthy increase, but not the adult portion the Supermono would need to run with the Austrian Rotax or kitted Japanese engines in the popular Sound of Singles class. So a 4.4-mm increase in bore and 2-mm increase in stroke brought the displacement to 549-cc and a claimed 75 horsepower. The liquid-cooled engine, with belt-driven dual overhead cams and four desmo valves, had computerized twin fuel injection, 12:1 compression, and a six-speed transmission. The Supermono, gassed up, weighed 300 pounds and was smack-yourself-in-the-forehead beautiful.

Designer Pierre Terblanche had dressed the tidy chassis in a red sharkskin suit, with a supple fairing that

Fearsome Carl Fogarty, the tarmac shark of Blackburn, Lancashire, Isle of Man absolute record-holder, dusted the factory boys at Donnington in 1992 as a privateer. As Ducati's lead rider in 1993 he had to settle for second place behind Russell, which focused his gaze even more tightly.

left the trellis frame partially visible. The tank combined sharp lines and graceful contours, and the cantilevered carbon fiber tail section incorporated a spoiler and minimalist seat cushion. The appointments included titanium engine covers and top triple clamp, carbon fiber fender/fork shield, side panels, airbox, and instrument nacelle, Marchesini wheels, bridged aluminum swingarm, and fully adjustable Ohlins suspension. Tasty. The Supermono had the most-frankly aggressive profile of any roadster yet built, arguably the best aerodynamics, and almost certainly the highest price for a single, $30,000. The top speed was 141 miles per hour.

Don Canet, *Cycle World* road test editor, rode the Supermono at Willow Springs Raceway in 1993. "Without a doubt, the Supermono was the sharpest-handling Ducati I'd ever ridden," he said. "We had it out at Willow for a day; it was agile and stable and a ton of fun. It felt like it had unlimited cornering clearance; and it got around there good, 3 or 4 seconds under the current singles class record at the track."

The contemporary neo-thumper created significant buzz, equal in intensity if not demography to the enthu-

siastic reception for the Monster. Ducati had not invented the factory hot rod—Cyclone of Minneapolis was building cafe racers in 1914—but Bologna had kept the tradition alive consistently for more than 30 years. Cagiva floated intentions of offering a street-legal version but it never came to pass. The company's expansion plans already showed signs of over-optimism. Priorities were necessarily given to the upcoming 916 and the Monster, both of which represented greater profit potential than the projected figures for a road-ripping single. The Supermono would carry on as a limited production racer for qualified privateers. Rumors of a road version persist still.

Pierre Terblanche had been captivated by Ducatis in the mid-1970s. "Cook Neilson's victory at Daytona, to me that was a big moment," he said. "I thought they were the best bikes ever. My first street bike was a 750 GT that someone had modified. I worked at Volkswagen and did cars, experimental interiors mainly, but I just wanted to do bikes, that was my passion. So I applied in Italy, made some models and went to Aprilia and Ducati, and Tamburini employed me and here I am.

"My work started with the Paso, with the spoiler on top and raising the fairing a bit; then came the 888 Ducati, and then I went to Varese where my first project

The brute-cruiser created a mammoth market for factory and aftermarket accessories, and customized Monsters soon roamed the land. Wayne Harrison's colorful creature combines 1950s-style hot rod flames with carbon fiber bits and pieces hither and yon, including the mufflers.
Tod Rafferty

Many people were surprised, even shocked, by the Monster. Quite a few fled into the streets seeking a dealership where they could buy one, which they did in significant numbers. Some of the more traditional Ducatisti viewed this trend with alarm, but had to admit it was a cute beast.

The Supermono was an instant hit, for both the innovative engineering of Bordi and Domenicali and Terblanche's stylish and purposeful bodywork. Rumors of impending production versions for the road have been floating for more than seven years, but haven't materialized. **Nick Cedar**

was the Supermono. After that I did the Canyon 600 and 900 for Cagiva. The first one I was really happy with was the Mono. I had no constraints at all, people just said it had to be red and beautiful and ready for Munich. That was in about three months. We did the model making ourselves; the rear subframe, the steering head was waisted, so the air could come past there. We had to

make modifications to get the fuel-injectors sitting right with the airbox, pushing it forward like the 916.

"The Mono and the 916 were done at the same time, and I wasn't working with Tamburini anymore, and they were almost done in parallel. The Supermono came out before the 916, but I don't know if it had much influence on the 916. We also did the 900 SS in three months, from

Racing success for the Supermono was immediate in Europe and the United States, with singles-only classes proliferating. Jeff Nash of Advanced Motor Sports and Silverman Museum Racing won the Sound of Singles titles in 1997 and 1998. Here he hustles his Supermono around Sears Point. **Tod Rafferty**

start to finish. Not really three months, of course, when you figure that you're working an average of 17 1/2 hours a day, seven days a week. So it was three calendar months, but in work hours more like seven months."

In 1993 the 888 SP lost its trick Ohlins fork, which was replaced by a Showa unit, but the engine gained goodies from the SPS model. The big valves, Corsa intake cams, and twin fuel injectors bumped the horsepower, and the electronics were upgraded likewise. A steel container supplanted the carbon fiber fuel tank, but the fibrous mufflers remained. The SPO, a Stateside version of the Strada, had smaller valves, milder cams, single injectors, and was about 15 pounds heavier.

Cagiva/Ducati had reason to celebrate the 1993 season. The heralded 916, after two years' development, was ready for the road and track; the Monster was a huge success worldwide; John Kocinski had won the U.S. Gran Prix at Laguna Seca in convincing fashion; and Doug Polen captured the U.S. Superbike championship with Ferracci. Plus, the motorcycle market in the States was again on a growth curve, and although sportbike sales had fallen slightly, cruisers were swinging upward.

Good news was not in evidence when the U.S. season opened at Daytona. Eddie Lawson, unretired for a guest ride on injured Jamie James' Vance & Hines

Yamaha, won a fierce battle with Scott Russell on the Muzzy Kawasaki. Polen's Ducati suffered tire and fuel-consumption problems, finishing far afield. All of which was shadowed darkly by a seventh-lap accident that took the life of Jimmy Adamo. In turn six, exiting the infield, the Ducati's front brakes apparently failed and sent the 36-year-old racing veteran into the haybales and a concrete wall. He died instantly.

The racing community was struck dumb. Adamo and Reno Leoni had been fixtures on the American road-racing scene for more than 20 years; they had won the Battle of the Twins Championship three years running, in 1981, 1982, and 1983; Jimmy had compiled 32 wins in the class and was well liked among the fans and his fellow racers. The two men had been instrumental in establishing and maintaining Ducati's competition presence in the United States, even during times when Ducati had little commercial identity in the American market. Adamo was survived by his wife, Melanie, and two young daughters. Leoni was devastated.

"I didn't really take it so easily," he recalls, "because we were together for so long. He was the only rider who could stay a long time . . . and we could do things together without fighting or having different ideas. I really liked Jimmy.

"I can't really say what happened, but I think it was the front brakes. He was running his own team then, and he had just come back from Italy. He bought all the new stuff—brakes, forks, tank—and he paid for everything. Knowing Jimmy, the way he felt, I think the brakes failed and he tried to save the bike, instead of pitching

The singular racing purpose of the Supermono is apparent in its specifications, appearance, and sound. The lightweight frame (13 pounds), lots of carbon fiber, and 10,000 rpm 572-cc engine speak pure performance. But a street-legal, 600-cc, electric-start Supermono SS is not unlikely. Domani. Tod Rafferty

The 916 made its first appearance in 1995, accompanied by a 748-cc sibling. Although it was developed directly from the 888, the 916 displayed numerous engineering and design changes, most visibly the single-sided, cast-aluminum swingarm. And it was lighter and faster.

In 1994 the 900 Superlight regained the inverted Ohlins fork and full-floating Brembo front brakes of the originals, and was available in red or yellow with full or half fairing. Models shown here are fitted with carbon fiber mufflers and the earlier Marvic composite wheels. Nick Cedar

The fast-growing list of rapid Aussies added the name Mat Mladin in 1993, when he campaigned the Cagiva 500-cc Grand Prix two-stroke. Although his performance didn't match the widely disseminated pre-season hype, Mladin later achieved greater success in Superbike racing. Tod Rafferty

The 916 SP had slightly higher compression, titanium connecting rods, two injectors per cylinder rather than one, and larger valves. This engine made about 20 horsepower more than the standard version. The SP had Ohlins suspension at both ends, and was good for 160 miles per hour.

down the bike, and he went straight. I think he tried to save it because of all the money he had put into that bike. That was a very hard thing, because he had come in before and complained that the brake fluid was coming up from the master cylinder. I don't really know if that's what failed, but that's what I thought."

Leaving on the 916

Despite Cagiva's success-builders in Superbike racing and the broad acceptance of the Elefant, 900 SS, and Monster, little professional marketing attention had been applied to the American market in the same period. The distributor-dealership framework had deteriorated under revolving management teams and political in-fighting, and dealers were not happy with Bologna's pricing policies, for which they absorbed losses on discounted and unsold parts. The customers were growing increasingly moody with the waiting periods for both parts and current models, and the sportbike market was shrinking in the bargain. All this just as the ballyhooed 916 was poised to appear, and with it a 748-cc sibling equipped with the same tasty bits. And this just as Ducati's major component suppliers began to register their concerns about unpaid invoices and repeated promises. Communications between Bologna and Varese had developed a brittle quality.

These problems were not apparent on the showroom floors. The 1994 900 SS had an upgraded Showa fork, reinforced swingarm, and remote brake and clutch reservoirs, with wheels and frames painted in matching bronze. Two new versions of the Supersport were configured specifically for the U.S. market in 1994, the 900 CR econo-cafe racer and the 900 SP. At $7,600, the CR achieved cost-effectiveness with a steel swingarm, non-

adjustable fork, narrower rear wheel, and plastic fenders. The full fairing, remote reservoirs, and floating front brakes were also absent. The CR undercut the price of a Honda VFR750 by $600, and was $2,100 below the SP. The 900 Sport Production was the Stateside rendition of the Superlight, with a dual seat, carbon fiber fenders and clutch cover, and limited-edition number plate. All 900-cc models remained relatively unchanged through 1996. The spotlight now shone on the 916.

Designed to go into battle against Honda's equally heralded RC 45, the new Ducati would have to be lighter, narrower, shorter, and faster. Tamburini's experience with Gran Prix racers was applied throughout the planning and engineering of the 916, with emphasis on the centralization of mass. The twin's higher center of balance made it slower to change directions than most other designs, a problem the designer addressed by reducing both the wheelbase and steering head angle. This required tilting the engine forward 1.5 degrees to allow clearance for the front tire, and helped shift needed weight bias to the front end. The chassis emerged with a 55.5-inch wheelbase, nearly an inch shorter than the 888, and a steering head adjustable from 24 to 25 degrees. An aluminum rear subframe carried the seat/tail section and saved weight.

The highlight of the 916 chassis was the cast-aluminum, single-sided swingarm, handsome and functional despite its necessary weight. Supplied by Brembo, the mono-lever attached in traditional Ducati fashion to the engine cases, but also through the frame for another measure of rigidity. An adjustable Showa shock absorber and 43-mm inverted fork suspended everything in amiable fashion at uncommon speeds, although the shock was under-damped for enjoyment of full-tilt boogeying. The fork, on the other hand, provided inspiring compliance at serious velocities and added a wide range of adjustment.

Although playing junior varsity to the 916, the 748 proved to be an effective tool in its own right. The little brother was built for European Supersport racing against 600-cc fours, and Michael Paquay won the division in 1995. Fabrizio Pirovano repeated the feat in 1996.

Engineers Massimo Bordi and Luigi Mengoli added 2 mm of stroke to bring the 888 to 916-cc, with 11:1 compression, and single injectors per four-valve desmo head. The engine made 105 horsepower at 9,000 rpm in standard trim, and another 12 or so in the following SP version at 10,700. At 460 pounds, the production 916 was good for mid-10s in the quarter-mile and a top speed close to 160 miles per hour. The closest thing yet

What was to be a limited edition signature model became a commemorative piece when Italian Formula One racing hero Ayrton Senna was killed at Imola. An initial run of 300, in metallic charcoal with red wheels, appeared in 1995. The series was continued in 1997 with a light gray finish.

to a street-legal production roadracer, the 916 carried a list price of $14,500. *Cycle World* awarded the new Ducati its Bike of the Year laurels.

Even though the 916 had the benefit of three years' development, the process was more intermittent than linear. Tamburini's work was divided between the 916 and the Cagiva Gran Prix effort as shifting priorities dictated. As a result, only four factory racers were ready for the 1994 season: two for factory riders Fogarty and Falappa, one for Fabrizio Pirovano on the Davide Tardozzi team, and another for Jamie Witham of Britain's Moto Cinelli. In American Superbike, Troy Corser's FBF Ducati carried the older 888 chassis with a 955-cc engine. The racing engines were enlarged to compensate for the diminishing weight ratio between the twins and fours. At the end of 1993, the AMA had upped the minimum weight for twins from 309 to 335 pounds, and dropped the fours from 363 to 355. In May of 1994, at midseason, they threw out the 20-pound differential altogether and set the minimum at 355 for both twins and fours.

The 916's bodywork showed the obvious influence of Terblanche's Supermono. Airscoops were incorporated below the headlights to feed the new, larger airbox, and mufflers tucked under the tail section improved aerodynamics at the rear. The new Ducati established high marks for design and performance, and even those veteran Ducatisti who had succumbed to skepticism over the Cagiva conglomeration had to admit that the 916 was really something. Here was a unified piece of high-performance moto-sculpture with fit and finish to match its functional capabilities, and the shape, sound, and Italian flash to make it an instant classic.

With the 916 the collaborative efforts of Ducati and Cagiva blossomed in full measure. Bologna had gained the benefits of nearly 10 years of relative economic security, expanded production, innovative engineering, bold styling, and improved distribution. The Castiglionis had developed Cagiva into the world's fifth largest motorcycle manufacturer, and had won Superbike championships and 500-cc Grand Prix races. They had saved Ducati from itself, and the government, but had also spent lavishly and not always well. So the stage was set once again for Ducati to face the prospect of new owners and managers. Not an unfamiliar situation in Bologna; however, this time several buyers from outside Italy were interested.

Suited up and ready to swoop down upon his prey, the lanceman of Lancashire prepares for battle. Fogarty's frank reflections on the Stateside racing facilities created a minor firestorm of patriotic outrage, which led to lingering skirmishes of nationalistic invective conducted mostly in the motomedia. Tom Riles

In 1995 the scramblin' Louisianan Freddie Spencer returned to Superbike racing on a Fast By Ferracci Ducati. The former 250 and 500 Grand Prix champion won the fog-delayed rainy-day race at Laguna Seca. Here he is shadowed into the Corkscrew by teammate Tiger Sohwa. Bill McMillan

Stress Fractures

Cagiva's 500-cc two-stroke Gran Prix enterprise had financed the talents of Raymond Roche, Randy Mamola, Eddie Lawson, Giacomo Agostini, John Kocinski, Kel Carruthers, Doug Chandler, and a young Aussie named Mat Mladin. Several of these employees earned sizeable salaries, and adding a small Roman army of engineers and technicians made this a more than moderately expensive program. Plus, a European revival of popularity for motor scooters had cut into Cagiva's market share in two-stroke econo-motorcycles. Some would suggest, and others openly charge, that Ducati's international Superbike success and corresponding sportbike sales were providing the primary funding for Cagiva's GP failure. Undeterred, the Castiglionis announced the intention of entering a Ferrari-designed 750-cc four in World Superbike racing the following season. This was not to happen. The traditional collision between emotional Italian causes and the ministers of finance was imminent.

John Kocinski did win the 1994 season-opening Australian GP, blitzing the Japanese teams and posting Cagiva's first heads-up victory on a dry track. Little John of Little Rock, Arkansas, had won three straight American 250-cc championships, and took the world title in 1990 with Roberts Yamaha. In 1991 he advanced to the 500 class as Wayne Rainey's teammate, but had difficulties with the more powerful bikes. While his abilities as a gifted rider were widely acknowledged, Kocinski's growing reputation as a temperamental smartass tended to eclipse his substantial talents. Although he finished third

Freddie Spencer had poor luck at Laguna in the World Superbike event, finishing seventh in the first round and dropping out of the second with a broken gearbox. Fast Freddie later opened his own racing school in Las Vegas, and became a roadracing commentator for the Speedvision network. **Tom Riles**

With Fogarty jumping to Honda, Ducati fielded the formidable team of Troy Corser, John Kocinski, and Pierfrancesco Chili in 1996. Kocinski and Gobert shared wins at Laguna Seca, but Corser's two second-place finishes put him in the point lead for the championship. **Bill McMillan**

in points for 1992, the 25-year-old racer left the Roberts camp to ride for the Suzuki 250 Grand Prix team.

The parting was less than harmonious. Kocinski complained that not only did Rainey's program get far more attention than his, but that his contract with manager Gary Howard represented a conflict of interest, since Howard also represented team owner Kenny Roberts. "I was in a mafia," Kocinski claimed in a *Cycle World* interview. "How is it possible for your manager to be your manager when he is also working for the team owner? It's a total conflict of interest. Is that even legal?"

Although he had finished third at Assen, Kocinski's bike expired on the cool-off lap and he missed the podium ceremonies. Accused of purposely blowing up his engine and avoiding the podium, Kocinski was fired by Suzuki. His subsequent four-race deal with Cagiva led to a victory on the 500 at Laguna Seca; while leading the Spanish GP, he crashed avoiding a falling rider. In 1994, though, no more wins followed Australia, and Kocinski finished well and ended third in points. He and teammate Doug Chandler were second and third to Mick Doohan at the Argentinian Gran Prix.

Chandler, the softspoken wrangler from Salinas, California, was U.S. Superbike champion on a Honda in 1990 and had confirmed his GP skills with Suzuki in 1992. The Cagiva years added a champion-of-lost-causes element to his character, which he would carry over to Harley-Davidson's struggling Superbike program in 1995. Chandler rode well on the Cagiva, and had praise for its capability. "The biggest thing was that the straightaway speed was down a bit, but it wasn't that bad," he said. "They had made a lot of progress over the years with different riders on it, and the handling was pretty good. In '94 Johnny and I were both on the podium in Argentina, and I thought that was an accomplishment.

"They just figured that the streetbike, which I guess is now going to be released as an MV Agusta, was what they wanted to pursue. I think they thought they would get something back out of it, rather than just the glamor of Grand Prix."

The 955, racing brother of the 916, proved its mettle in winning Carl Fogarty's World Superbike Championship title. With its additional 2 mm of stroke, the engine made genuine ass-kicking midrange and better than 130 horsepower at the macadam. Bigger valves, titanium rods, and 11.6:1 pistons allowed the V-twin to spin 12,000 rpm, and the bike came off corners with notable velocity. Unfortunately it didn't steer so well. Weight bias was still a problem, prompting a mid-year switch to a

longer swingarm and more steering head angle, and the factory teams were chasing suspension settings for most of the season. In the United States, Ferracci and Troy Corser, newest of the railin' Australians, won the Superbike class with an updated year-old machine.

Leaving Cagiva

Ducati's certitude about the 916 was certified by the appearance of a 748-cc rendition in 1995. Previous down-sized sporties had not set any sales records in the United States, but the 748 was permitted to race with 600-cc fours in the European Supersport series. The significant selling point for American riders was the selling point, nearly $3,000 less than a 916. And the good stuff was still there: 916 cams, 43-mm Showa fork, four-piston Brembo brakes, mono-lever swingarm, all encased in screaming yellow bodywork. While not a torque-monster like the 916, the 748 made nearly the same power at higher rpm and was a joy to ride.

For those devoted to the light-heavyweight class, and willing to ante up more money, the 748 SP offered cams good for another 6 horsepower with a smidgeon more compression, an Ohlins rather than Showa rear damper, an aluminum rear subframe, and Termignoni carbon fiber mufflers. Add cast-iron fully-floating Brembo discs and braided steel brake lines and *voila*, a Euro Supersport for the backroads of America. Nearly the same dollars would buy a 916, but for many riders weaned on Triumph, Nortons, and Ducati 750 Sports, this was the displacement God intended twins to have. Bigger, in many cases, was not necessarily better.

In a related size matter, the Monster also came available with either a 900-, 750-, or 600-cc engine. The market reception for the M series was still on a growth

Kocinski, followed by Gobert and Corser, collected a fairly easy win in the first heat after Gobert crashed while leading. Colin Edwards had been expected to do well with the Honda on his home track, but could only manage fourth place. Fogarty's bike problems put him eleventh. Bill McMillan

John Kocinski was determined to repeat his victory in the second round, and Gobert was equally interested in seeing that he didn't. Corser held the early lead, but Little John and The Go show got by and away. On the last lap Kocinski's engine quit, granting Corser second behind Gobert. **Bill McMillan**

The Monster fuel tank had become a steel canvas for all manner of striking graphic representations, few more appropriate than the illustrated desmo valve gear. Given the moderate price and its elastic platform for the decorative arts, the Monster accounted for nearly a third of all Ducatis sold. **Tod Rafferty**

curve, and the catalog of parts and accessories from Ducati and aftermarket firms was expanding accordingly.

The 1995 World Superbike season shaped up as another intense tussle between Fogarty and Muzzy Kawasaki pilot Scott Russell. Instead, the Ducatis dominated the early races and Russell quit Kawasaki to go GP racing with Lucky Strike Suzuki. The move caught Rob Muzzy by surprise, since Russell still had two years to go on his contract. As a result, Fogarty's most serious competition was provided by U.S. Superbike champion Troy Corser on the Promotor Racing Ducati, with occasional parries from Honda riders Aaron Slight and Simon Crafar. Fogarty dominated the series and won his second championship for Ducati, but he still entertained hopes of riding in the GP showcase. At 29 the fire in his belly still burned, but Fogarty knew the odds against him grew with the passage of time. His ensuing availability was common knowledge, but the only serious offer came from Honda to ride the 1996 RC45 in World Superbike. And Carl Fogarty accepted, citing the need for a new challenge, and hoping the next hop would be to Grand Prix 500-cc two-strokes.

In the United States a former Grand Prix champion returned to Superbike racing. Three-time world champ

Freddie Spencer joined Mike Smith and Takahiro Sowha on the Ferracci team, while former *Ferraccista* Pascal Picotte jumped to Muzzy Kawasaki. The game of musical saddles grew more engaging and important each year, as Superbike gained in worldwide popularity and created more marketing opportunities for riders. Grand Prix was still the big show for the major dough, but few seats were ever available, while Superbike salaries and contingency money were ascending. Salary ratios between GP and Superbike had closed rapidly, although sponsor contingencies remained far higher in the Grand Prix arena. As the financial disparities shrank, though, some riders for whom GP had been the holy grail began to reconsider the career benefits in Superbike racing.

The Ferracci team had their hands full with the Smokin' Joe's Hondas ridden by Miguel DuHamel and Mike Hale. Smith rode the Ducati to third, but DuHamel was dominant in winning Honda's first Superbike title in seven years. Louisiana's Freddie Spencer took a heart-warming victory at a rain-soaked Laguna Seca, postponed by fog from Sunday to Monday and attended by almost nobody but the participants and a few determined photographers. Honda had recognized, or remembered, the marketing importance of racing in the American sportbike demographic, demonstrably illustrated by Ducati's resurgence. In Honda's broad racing spectrum, only World Superbike showed lack of strength, which they addressed by hiring Fogarty.

Relieving Cagiva

Ducati's racing plans for 1996, and its engineering, design, production, and marketing intentions as well, were unsettled by Cagiva's economic straits. Hindsight, in its characteristic clarity, reveals that Cagiva was simply unprepared for Ducati's success. They had overestimated their abilities to compete in two international racing campaigns, develop and market their own brand models as well as those of Husqvarna, and have sufficient reserves to ride out a prolonged dip in the market. And who could have predicted the rebirth of the scooter trade? After all, this was Italy. The Castiglionis had scrambled to bring Ducati production up to speed, but had to borrow money to do so. And when payments to outside suppliers of components began falling past due, Cagiva faced the loss of its most successful brand. Suppliers refused to fill further Ducati orders until the bills were paid; workers were laid off at the factory; taxes were due. Word of a distress sale reached the international grapevine.

The letter designation brands the 900 FE as the Final Edition of the 1991–1997 SS series. The limited edition (800) Superlight featured silver bodywork, black wheels, and a high-rise exhaust system. Although a largely cosmetic commemorative, the moderate numbers made the FE an instant collectible.

Two of the most serious inquiries came from the United States. Sam Zell, a Chicago financier with a taste for Ducatis, was the first to express strong interest, but negotiations fell short of expectations on both sides. The Texas Pacific Group (TPG), specialists in multinational mergers and acquisitions, was next at the table. TPG holdings included Del Monte Foods, Continental Airlines, Virgin Entertainment, and various interests in communications, wine, clothing, health care, and waste management—virtually the full spectrum of human activity except for motorcycles. With Germany's Deutsche Bank Morgan Grenfell as a financial partner, TPG inspected Ducati's production facilities, company history, and current capabilities. They found a willing workforce, capable engineers

Ducati's first official sport-touring model arrived in 1997. The ST2 mixed chassis components from the 888 and 916, with a 944-cc engine derived from the earlier 907 IE. With the saddlebags removed, the mufflers could be raised slightly for an added measure of ground clearance. Nick Cedar

The ST2 was preceded by one of the most elaborate promotional campaigns in Ducati history. Compared to most sport-touring mounts on the market, the Ducati rendition put the most emphasis on the sporting side. Speedier sport-tourists would await the ST4 with its 916-based engine.

and designers, a strong racing tradition, and a good product in demand internationally at premium prices. The only two missing components were money and management.

The money, a reported $43 million for 49 percent of the company, satisfied the outstanding debts, hired more workers, and bought new production equipment. Within two months Ducati was up and running again, with Massimo Bordi remaining as general manager and technical director, and Federico Minoli as managing director. Minoli was part of the TPG team that negotiated the acquisition from Cagiva. A former national manager for Benetton in Canada, South America, and the United States, Minoli worked for the consulting firm of Bain & Company of Boston.

"I was working as a due diligence and turnaround manager," Minoli says, "looking at companies and deciding which were worth buying. TPG called about doing something with Ducati, helping with the negotiations and dealing with 'these weird Italian brothers,' the Castiglionis. I happened to know the Castiglionis—I was born near Varese—and I was therefore a facilitator.

"These were people who had worked to build their company; for them it was much more like losing a child, not just a matter of making or losing money. It took me from November of '95 to May '96 to convince them to agree to a letter of intent. In May we got the exclusivity, and I brought to Bologna 10 people who had 45 days to

determine whether the company was sound; we talked to dealers, suppliers, managers, looked at the books. Our conclusion was that Ducati was a great company, but there was really no company. There was a great product, history, racing, and an R&D department.

"We made our recommendations, and in October, TPG bought 51 percent of Ducati. Then we started building the company around the product and the history. In 1997 we reached an all-time record for production, sales, registrations, and profits.

"That was the great moment of Massimo Bordi, frankly. All I did was sign $70 million in checks. Bordi was able to quickly restore relations with suppliers, and hire about 300 people. Many of the people did not really trust Ducati anymore. Most of the new workers were young people, and 30 percent were female. We also had to decide immediately where to invest the money. Manufacturing quality and safety were at the top of the list. The testing benches didn't meet emission requirements; we replaced obsolete equipment for crankcases and cylinder heads, and installed electronically controlled bolting machines."

Minoli modestly described the process as fairly simple. "Management 101, really. We just took the top 20 problems and addressed them in order." The unreliable alternator, from neighbor Ducati Elettrotechnica was available on credit; for the Japanese Nippondenso unit one paid in advance. Mahle pistons from Germany were expensive, but reliable. Next on the agenda were restructuring plans for distribution and marketing. The new team, most of them young Italian, American, and British employees, moved quickly with outlines to restore the marque to health and prosperity.

Minoli admits that Ducati has been and will continue as a niche player in the motorcycle market, but that there is room for expansion within the genre. His favorite diagram divides the industry into four categories: Performance, Lifestyle, Comfort, and Function, arranged clockwise on the four points of the compass. Within a large circle in the center is Japan, covering a good portion of all classifications. Minoli pencils Harley-Davidson into the southeast segment, combining Comfort and Lifestyle. Ducati resides in the northwest section of the chart, incorporating portions of Performance and Function. "The Japanese are all over the place," Minoli says. "We will never go head to head with them."

What Ducati would do was much like what Harley-Davidson had done a decade earlier: to expand the boundaries of their own niche; to stay

A large measure of the Monster's success derived from its attraction for female riders. The low seat height and relatively moderate price made it a popular choice, particularly with those of shorter stature or lighter wallets. Add a set of saddlebags and you have an instant sport-touring cruiser. Bill McMillan

The 916/996 and Supermono are obvious choices for the racetrack, but the Monster and its 888-derived frame are not necessarily unsuitable for competition. Steve Midgley of Salt Lake Motorsports demonstrates the race-cruiser's carving chops at Sears Point Raceway.
Tod Rafferty

Monsters are rarely spotted racing on unpaved surfaces, but some enthusiasts are willing to try anything. Here Stevie Smith of Beaudry Motorsports in Coeur d'Alene, Idaho, touches down from the Super TT jump at California's Buttonwillow Raceway. Note the added subframe in front of the engine. Nick Cedar

within their traditional performance and function roles, but to broaden the definitions and attract customers who might otherwise pass on cutting edge sportbikes. The Monster had nudged Ducati into the periphery of the Lifestyle segment and enticed more female riders, while still exhibiting the basic elements of high-performance equipment. The sport-touring ST2, announced in 1994 and delayed by Cagiva's cash flow dilemma, was on the way to extend the model profile in another dimension. The 916 was on line in standard, factory racing, and customer racing renditions. The new 900 SS, restyled by Pierre Terblanche to replace the aging model introduced in 1991, was coming along and Troy Corser won the 1996 World Superbike Championship on the Promotor Ducati. The company had money in the bank, and the good times were rolling in Bologna.

Understandably, no distinctly new models were on the immediate horizon. "I am not controlling Pierre," Minoli says, " but we won't all of a sudden come out with a cruiser. Harley-Davidson and us are the only two brands that have such character and distinct personality that we can build a world around it. Harley did it already, and did it beautifully. We haven't done it yet, so our way to grow will be to build this thing, and the first moves will be as close to the bike as possible."

With the TPG acquisition came concerns among enthusiasts that Ducati's racing program might be trimmed severely. "Absolutely not," replied Minoli. "They have not reduced the racing budget. We may want to make the racing department more efficient; worldwide there are about 40 teams that race with Ducati. But we really only assist three—Vance and Hines, Ferracci, and Ducati Performance—to the other 37 we sell bikes. We might do something like Honda Racing Corporation, have a 24-hour hotline that would connect independent teams with the factory."

Minoli was offered the CEO position within a year of the acquisition, his initial reluctance buffered by an appealing package of stock options. A former Moto Guzzi rider, Minoli doesn't fit the profile of an average suit from

Mat Mladin jumped from the Yoshimura Suzuki to the Fast By Ferraci Ducati in 1997, and won the opener at Phoenix. Although he went on to collect three more victories, Mladin had to settle for third on the season. Doug Chandler took his third title, despite winning only one race. Bill McMillan

the corporate boardroom. He nows rides an ST2 and is a regular at the pit wall during World Superbike events, where he gladly shares in the celebration when Ducati riders win. Given the frequency of this occasion, this is a man happy in his work.

Superbikes and Saddle Pals

Honda fully intended to end this Ducati nonsense in 1996. Ducati's weight advantage was history, Honda had the certified talents of Carl Fogarty and Kiwi Aaron Slight, and the RC45 was in its third generation of development. Still wickedly fast, with better midrange, the V-4 also remained a handful on anything but smooth surfaces. Honda pinned its hopes on Fogarty finding the proper equation to sort out the combined issues of weight distribution, steering, and suspension. Ducati hired the intermittently brilliant John Kocinski, 1994 American Superbike champion Troy Corser of Australia, and popular 250 GP contender Pierfrancesco Chili from Bologna.

Added to this ultimate shootout showdown were two more young guns: the 21-year-old racing sensation from Australia, Anthony Gobert, on a Muzzy Kawasaki, and promising Texas dirt-tracker turned roadracer Mike Hale, 23, aboard a Promotor team Ducati from the factory. Honda's fortunes dimmed early when Fogarty broke his wrist in practice and, before the third round at Hockenheim, Honda fired his long-time mechanic and confidant Anthony "Slick" Bass. Foggy went on to win the second race in Germany, but it would be one of only four over the season.

Corser served notice in the second round at Donnington, breaking the lap record set by Kevin Schwantz in 1991 on a GP Suzuki, and won both legs. But by midseason at Laguna Seca, Slight held a 45-point lead on Corser. When the Aussie came second twice in California, behind Kocinski and Gobert, he gained a 4-point edge heading back to Europe. Fogarty was back to form at Assen and won two fierce contests with Corser, Gobert, Kocinski, and Slight. With two races left in the season, he also announced that he would return to Ducati in 1997. When Slight crashed at Phillip Island, Corser locked up the title for Ducati, despite being taken out of the second race by a strafing seagull.

Given the Cagiva upheaval, Ducati no longer had the wherewithal for a top shelf effort in American Superbike. Dauntless Doug Chandler had returned to Muzzy Kawasaki, and the title race was again distilled to a battle

Cook Neilson (left) and Phil Schilling joined the California Hot Rod for a 1997 reunion at Daytona International Speedway. Only the 1974 Super Sport showed no visible signs of age, as it had been in storage for 20 years. Tom Riles

Neilson wore his original leathers in honor of the occasion, but opted for a more contemporary full-coverage helmet. Rider and bike were still a good fit also, and Cook was certain to dial up some thunderous nostalgia on the banking. Old Blue recently passed to its third owner and now lives in New Jersey. Tom Riles

Carl Fogarty powers out to the edge of the stutter bumps entering the long straightaway at Laguna Seca. The Briton had to subdue his dislike of the Monterey circuit to stay with John Kocinski on the Castrol Honda. He made the pace, which was good enough for second in both heats.
Bill McMillan

between him and Honda's defending champion, Miguel DuHamel. Ferracci had the young dirt-tracker Larry Pegram and Harley TwinSport rider Shawn Higbee. Chandler trailed DuHamel by two points going into the last race in Las Vegas, but rode masterfully to win his second championship. Mat Mladin, fourth overall on a Yoshimura Suzuki, was signed to ride a Ferracci Ducati for the following year.

During the ensuing silly season of seat swaps and contract talks, Kocinski slipped away to sign with Castrol Honda, thus eliminating the worry of pronouncing his Ducati sponsor's name, Kremlyovskaya Vodka. Little John effectively swapped seats with Fogarty, who returned to Ducati and teamed up with Frankie Chili. Troy Corser decided to make his Grand Prix move with Yamaha, and Scott Russell came back from the GP wars to ride a Yamaha with Colin Edwards. The AMA Superbike roster changed little for 1997, and again feature the showdown between Doug Chandler's Kawasaki and the Honda of Miguel DuHamel. Vance & Hines switched from Yamaha to Ducati, with Thomas Stevens in the

saddle. Another young American charger, Ben Bostrom, made his Superbike debut on an American Honda.

Back to Business

Relieved of its financial nightmares, Ducati returned to serious business in 1997. The timing was fortuitous, since Honda and Suzuki had both decided to build V-twins aimed directly at Italians' traditional market. Honda's VTR 1000, showing obvious 900 SS design influences, and the Suzuki TL1000S, impinging on 916 territory, were both created to contest Ducati's sportbike domain. Not on the track, where the Japanese would stick with their four-cylinder entries for the time being, but on the back roads, American byways especially. Neither of the new 90-degree, double overhead-cam V-twins, with bore and stroke identical to the Ducati Superbike, were in the same league for handling at the edge. But both offered a measure of the Italian style, and posted premiums of reliability and price.

The people at Ducati were, by turns, flattered, amused, dismissive, and concerned by the Japanese contestants. Bologna would never be able to compete with Honda or Suzuki on price points, but they retained the status conferred by originality, international racing championships, and the exclusivity of Italian panache. Ducati created magazine ads with two images of the Mona Lisa, one's face showing Asian features, and the headline "Why have a copy when you can own the original?"

As it turned out, neither the Honda nor Suzuki would register as a serious threat to the 916. Ducati's racing twin was instilled with nearly a quarter-century of trial-and-error development. Not even Honda could synthesize that experience overnight. The 916 retained its edge for those who demanded the best in corner-strafing capability and intuitive handling, and who had no qualms about paying $6,000 more for the Ducati. The Japanese twins did, however, threaten the more conservative market segment for the 900 SS, which had remained largely unchanged for seven years. The carbon fiber front fender was now standard, yellow was added as an optional color, and several detail changes were made to the brakes. But the styling of the SS was similar to the 1991 version, and sales were down. The new model was scheduled for release in 1998. Again, in the Italian manner, it would naturally be late.

Ducati had expended considerable effort on the 748 program. The smaller twin was eligible to compete with 600-cc fours in the European Supersport championship,

The new 900 SS arrived to mixed reviews and stayed that way. The move to a more aggressive profile and riding position pleased some and disappointed others. Many who liked the styling simply opted for higher handlebars, while others enjoyed the more sporting stance and improved handling.

and Belgium's Michael Paquay had won seven of the eight rounds in 1995. Bologna saw a similar opportunity in AMA racing, where Miguel DuHamel was the dominant force on a Honda 600. But for 1997 the AMA decreed a 600-cc displacement maximum, regardless of engine configuration. In Europe, the FIM merely made the twins carry the same weight as the fours. Ducati-mounted Fabrizio Pirovano still won the division in 1996.

The 748 derived from the 916. With reduced centimeters, it also carried two fewer fuel injectors, and in stock trim was heavy and underpowered compared to the Japanese 600-cc fours. All of which made the AMA decision to disallow the Ducati in Supersport racing stick in a few craws, most prominently those of Eraldo Ferracci and Terry Vance. Both contended that the AMA had yielded to pressure from the Japanese manufacturers, a charge the association denied. AMA pro competition director Merrill Vanderslice told *Cycle World,* "When we've got an outstanding year of 600 Supersport racing at our doorstep right now, with four manufacturers ready to jump in, it really doesn't seem prudent to see if a bike that has

The 750 Supersport arrived in 1999 and—like the 900 SS—offered either the full or half fairing. The 750 lost about 16 horsepower to the 900, and about $2,000 off the price. Both models carried Weber-Marelli electronic fuel injection, with a single injector per cylinder.

more displacement could or could not compete." This came to be called the Dear Prudence rationale.

Ducati, meanwhile, was more concerned with the several important tasks at hand. One was the launch of the ST2, the first Bolognese sport-tourer, which had been on the back burner for three years. Designed by Monster-stylist Miguel Angel Galluzzi, the new sport-bagger proved to be more than just another parts-bin special. Compared to most other entries in this category, the ST2 put greater emphasis on the sport side of the spectrum, illustrated by the new 916-style frame.

Neither the ST2 engine nor running gear was merely warmed-over 900 SS components. The two-valve desmo system was common to both, but the ST2 engine gained liquid cooling, fuel injection, and 2-mm overbore, bringing displacement to 944-cc. With compression at 10.2:1, improved combustion chambers, chubby cams, lighter flywheels, and new ignition curve, the engine had both healthy midrange punch and substantial urge on up past 9,000 rpm. A tourist with an attitude.

The ST2 wouldn't win a corner-strafing contest with a 916, but it would carry two people in reasonable comfort for considerably greater distances. The chassis dimensions also reflected the sporting character of the new model; 56.3-inch wheelbase, 24-degree steering angle, and 4 inches of trail. Close to 916 specs, although the single-sided swingarm was deleted in favor of a twin-strut aluminum unit with rising-rate shock linkage. The Metzler radial-shod 17-inch wheels were suspended by Showa components at both ends, each adjustable for spring preload, compression, and rebound damping. Especially clever was the two-position muffler height adjustment, allowing saddlebag margins on the lower setting and more ground clearance on the top mount. Detractions included the stubby shift lever (later replaced), klutzy spring-loaded sidestand, and the lack of bungee cord hooks on the tail section.

Priced at $12,500, the ST2 represented a guarded step away from Ducati's hard-edged heritage of street-legal roadracers, but not a large step. The hallmark handling remained, and the convenience factors were sure to appeal to riders previously attracted to Ducati, but finally dissuaded by the lack of conveniences. The ST2 seemed the picture of demographic accuracy, destined to find acceptance in the contemporary modern world we live in today without fear of redundance. Sport-touring, however, remains a nebulous category. Broadly defined, it includes everything from four-, two-, or one-cylinder BMWs, a handful of Harleys, to a dozen or so Japanese fours and twins and several hybrid British Triumphs. A glory of multiple choices for riders, a crowded contest for small-volume manufacturers.

First unveiled at the Munich show in 1998, Pierre Terblanche's MH900e (Mike Hailwood evoluzione) grabbed plenty of attention. A later limited production (1,000) model was sold exclusively on the Internet.

The Monster, which had been a far riskier departure in terms of image, had paid off in spades, primarily because there was nothing else like it. And it was chummy. Sit on me, invited the Monster. Ride me around, you will like me. The Monster's style was its lack of contemporary style, which combined with its utility and price to make the engaging muscle-bobber popular worldwide. Galluzzi seemed to recognize that motorcycles could still be fun, that fashion and hyper-bike velocities were only a small part of the picture.

Thus, it was only logical to offer the Monster in 600- and 750-cc versions for even more moderate budgets, and obdurate insurance companies. The M750 achieved economies of transmission, offering five rather than the 900's six speeds, and retained the original Pantah wet clutch. With a less-adjustable fork, smaller front wheel, and single front disc brake, the 750 was less expensive than the 900, but retained the same rolling image of moto-industrial nudity. The Monster was well on its way to developing the most populous model roster in the Ducati lineup.

Using the same logic in the opposite direction, and more traditional Ducati style, Bologna served up the 916SPS. Having expanded the racing engine to 996-cc to compensate for the loss of their weight bonus, Bologna offered a limited run of 800 big-bore road-burners at $28,000 a piece. The cylinder head studs were moved out to accommodate the 4-mm larger cylinder, and the cases reinforced to withstand the increased power. With its lightened crank, Pankl rods, massaged heads, big valves, and dual 54-mm throttle bodies, the SPS made 12–15 more horsepower than the 916 and 6 foot-pounds more torque. Exhaling through enlarged Termingnoni carbon-fiber mufflers, the engine generated a prodigious baritone honk and an exhilarating midrange rush of race-style acceleration. Corner-exit speeds were stimulating. Only 50 examples of the SPS were allocated for U.S. dealers, although a few more found their way in by creative importation.

Back in the USA

Stateside racing wasn't Bologna's best playground in 1997. Ferracci had Mat Mladin in the saddle at Daytona and the only luck they had was hard. The outspoken Australian, who kept few of his distastes to himself, was vocally contempuous of the Florida circuit and was

Following Page
But for the tank and tail section shapes, the MHe bears little resemblance to the original Hailwood replica. The molded nylon fairing/tank is one piece; a single-sided tubular steel swingarm pivots in the crankcases. The finned oil sump is a cover.

Ben Bostrom trails Frankie Chili, as they both put the powers down coming out of the last turn at Laguna Seca. Gentleman Ben turned in impressive rides for a fourth and a third against the world's best, and went on to win the AMA series. For 2000 he joined Fogarty on the factory World team. Bill McMillan

In 1998, Fogarty's chances looked slim at midseason, but he hung in to win the title when Corser left Assen on a stretcher. **Bill McMillan**

rewarded with a bike that wouldn't start on the line. Mladin made three laps on his back-up bike and had to pit for an oil leak, then went back out and crashed. He did manage to win four races during the season, and ended third in the standings behind Chandler and DuHamel.

But 1997 was a good occasion for the previous generation, or two, with the reappearance at Daytona of Cook Neilson, Phil Schilling, and their 1977 winner, Old Blue. Superbike racing had undergone a few changes in 20 years, and the pair were on hand to honor the past and show the colors. Schilling, known to carry a high level of apprehension into the racing enterprise, fretted that the old 750 SS might fail to start, or just spit and fart its way around the track, or even shuck Neilson into the haybales. The rider, the former Clarence P. Noodleman, was simply happy to be at the track in the sunshine and still fit into his old leathers.

Owner Dale Newton, instrumental in Paul Ritter's Superbike program, had kept the overdog battlewagon more or less intact for two decades. Neilson was fairly sure it was the same machine, and at the re-introduction of bike and rider, when Dale's son Glen fired up the vintage racer, he was certain. "Because," he wrote in *Cycle World*, "20 years ago it spoke to me with a voice that was utterly its own, and now, as it sits all shimmer and grumble on its ancient oily wooden stool, a tiny motorcycle, really, a delicacy, it speaks to me with the same voice still, and I am moved to tears at the hearing of it."

Although the American Historic Racing Motorcycle Association had granted the assembled geezers only a three-lap "Parade of Greats," Neilson wasn't about to miss the opportunity to crank up the bass section for the benefit of Schilling and the assembled Ducatiophiles. And himself. Few sounds produced by internal combustion can match the bellow erupting from a heavy-breathing Ducati V-twin, especially on a speed-bowl echo chamber like Daytona, coincidentally Neilson's favorite track. So he dutifully opened the loud handle for the benefit of the vintage audience, and to remind himself just how sweet it was back then, up on the banking with the insistent wail of Wes Cooley's Suzuki fading behind him, cradled in the syncopated thunderstorm of a 10,000 rpm, 150-miles per hour Ducati twin. Twice, on the twice pipes if you please. Winning accompaniment then and now.

"The future? Ducati's prospects haven't changed," Neilson says today. "No one could ever understand the utterly Byzantine relationship between Ducati Motorcycles, Ducati Electronics, the Italian government, Ferrari, Bosch, Fiat, and a host of others. The last time I was there the banks were issuing their own currency, so go figure. I just have a feeling they'll be just fine, though, because even if they're not, they are—Italy being Italy."

World Superbike also delivered Ducati a dose of disappointment in 1997. Carl Fogarty was back after a one-season struggle with the Honda RC45, only to find a revised racer that was more difficult to ride. And John Kocinski was in the process of getting both the RC45 and his attitude dialed in. Fogarty had scored four wins on the Honda, which no one else had done, but found the RC45 still a serious handful on anything but smooth, flat circuits. The series quickly became a duel between the two British and American riders, with Aaron Slight and Colin Edwards in the mix, as well as Pierfrancesco Chili on a factory Ducati. Kocinski and Slight drew first blood at Phillip Island, Australia, with Fogarty taking a second and fourth.

By midseason the points race had contracted to a scratching struggle between Fogarty and Kocinski. Foggy

Troy Corser is trailed by the Yamaha of Noriyuki Haga, who made a daring pass on the penultimate lap to take round two at Laguna. Corser had won the first round and Fogarty managed only fifth. When he and Slight DNF the second heat, Corser's point lead made a sizeable jump. Bill McMillan

The moto-profile backdrop for the performing stage at Misano reflected Ducati's larger-than-life approach to World Ducati Weekend. Tod Rafferty

Part-time actor and full-time Ducatista Bobby Carradine was on hand as moderator for Speedvision's coverage of the big party. His own Roche Replica features a headlight decal that looks fairly realistic from a passing squad car.

Massimo Bordi was instrumental in both Ducati's technical reformation in the 1980s under Cagiva, and its subsequent economic revival a decade later with the TPG acquisition. He now serves as general manager and chief engineer, and rarely makes a point without an accompanying sketch. **Tod Rafferty**

had a 14-point lead going to Laguna Seca, but the Yank won both rounds with the Brit second twice, and the gap closed to 4 points. The pair split wins in Holland and the last round in Indonesia, but DNFs in England, Spain, and Japan put Fogarty into a distant second place at the end. On the last lap of the final event in Sentul, Kocinski took both himself and Kawasaki's Simon Crafar out with a crash, handing the win to Fogarty. The victory gave the Englishman second place in the series, edging out Aaron Slight. Kocinski's title made him the first rider to hold world championships in both Grand Prix and Superbike divisions.

Troy Corser had made the leap to GP racing in 1997, but would come back to Ducati after a disappointing season on the Promotor Yamaha YZR500. Anthony Gobert, the 22-year-old Aussie whizbang wonder-boy, also had difficulties in his debut with Lucky Strike Suzuki's Grand Prix team. Characteristically, Gobert was fast from the get-go, but a succession of broken collarbones, and his continuing image as a party-hearty hipster with a taste for beer and marijuana, dogged his steps. Gobert would slip down the food chain for 1998, back in U.S. Superbike on a Vance & Hines Ducati, where the fettucine would finally hit the fan. Mat Mladin would leave Ferracci for a three-year contract with Suzuki.

Nuevo 900 SS

In eight years the 900 SS had become the old gray mare of Ducati's sportbike stable, and was finally turned out to pasture. The philly sent in to replace her in the spring of 1998 was the Terblanche-styled Supersport, which defined a slightly different role for the venerable mainstay of the Ducati model roster. Elements of the Supermono style were apparent, but the new Supersport was more complex and less integrated.

With the ST2 in place, Ducati engineers and the new marketing mavens chose to move the Supersport closer to the 916 in terms of image, performance, and ergonomics. Sportier, in other words, but more civilized at the same time. The old 900 SS fit more accurately in the Grand Touring category, while the new Supersport was a more European-style sportbike—with quicker turning, better handling and braking, and a riding position closer to the racer's crouch. With a price differential of $5,000, the new SS became the working man's 916.

Similarities were in evidence. Only a few pounds heavier than its predecessor, the new Supersport gained 5 horsepower with the switch from carburetors to elec-

tronic fuel injection, and improved throttle response. With the wheelbase dropped to 54.9 inches, the steering head tucked in by a degree, and a tad less trail, the SS changed direction more quickly and accurately. The upgraded 43-mm Showa fork and slightly longer shock absorber furnished added stability at speed, especially on uneven roads. Lighter wheels and racing-pattern brakes likewise made aggressive deceleration a much more confident exercise. Functionally, it is a motorcycle superior on all counts to the model it replaced. The two prominent elements in the mixed reaction to the 900 Supersport were the riding position and the styling.

Part of Pierre Terblanche's design mission was to evoke the imagery of the original 750 SS of 1973. "I think we have eschewed trendiness and built on our tradition," he said. "Many of the styling cues obviously derive from the Supermono, but the bike design is essentially new. The dynamic grooves on the tank, the curves in the chassis, the play of light and shadow on the fairing, which serve to lighten the masses. . . . I didn't want all the hard edges of contemporary design. For me, it was all about voluptuous forms, organic shapes, curves. Look at the form of the bike, the way the shapes merge from front end to tank to tailpiece—it's one voluptuous shape."

While some sensualists, and several sybarites, agreed at the organic level, there was no immediate rush of customers willing to assume the racier riding position to gain the voluptuary image. Cristiano Silei, general manager at Ducati North America, is convinced the new design will eventually succeed. "I own one," he says. "The styling of this bike is new and different. When you change it's not easy for people to adapt, or even to understand it sometimes. I believe so much in this bike, I think in a few years it will become a classic. If the style doesn't appeal too much now, give it time. The more you look at the bike, the more you like it."

Designs of Future Past

"I can't say much about what we're doing," said Pierre Terblanche in 1998, " but I don't think you'll be disappointed in the bikes that are coming. Obviously we have to work on weight, aerodynamics, and simplicity, those are the main things. Because the bikes have become very complicated. In the 916 you have lots of wiring and tubes all over the place, and we're going to try and clean them up a little bit.

"I think the direction of design may change, and I think bikes will be even more functional. We are doing wind

tunnel testing now on all the production bikes, and all the future production bikes will have a lot of wind tunnel testing. We have to have a good idea of what's possible, within the design and styling constraints, because road motorcycles are not like Formula One cars; people still expect them to look like what they're used to. You can't build the best thing out there, because it might look very strange and nobody would want it. So we've got to build bikes that people understand, and have them go and look better, which is a tough one. Everybody's been told that the narrower bikes are, the better they go, when in fact it's the opposite way. Maybe you have to cover the rider sometimes, and not have him sticking out over the top.

"The race bike will have to be more aerodynamic; it's pointless having 15 horsepower more and going slower than the next guy. So there's a lot of work to be done; it might look different, maybe strange. To clean up

With new ownership came a team of young advertising and promotion people from the United States. The new ad campaign, shot in black and white by fashion photographer Ferdinando Scianna, featured Ducati employees. Kristin Schelter, then press officer, was later promoted to advertising manager.

Pierfrancesco Chili, former 250 Grand Prix rider, was the only Italian on the Ducati factory team in 1998. A national hero in Italy, Chili finished the season in fourth place in the point standings, but lost his ride when the company dropped the Virginio Ferrari–managed team for 1999.

people who think a high tail and a low front make things go like hell. It's actually the other way around.

"We also have the problem of the airbox and noise homologation. They say the Buell picked up 12 horsepower with the new airbox. Harley-Davidson can pass the noise regulations because they've got 35 horsepower, or whatever they have, but we can't get away with that. We have to have 80–85 horsepower, and we have to have 80 decibels. That's the single biggest problem, packaging for homologation, and making cannisters for California."

Racetrack Revenge

The AMA Superbike playbill for 1998 carried an engaging list of performers. Heading the list of players was the increasingly notorious Anthony Gobert, who had been canned by the Suzuki GP team for failing a drug test. The awesome Aussie was now on a Vance & Hines Ducati, the team generously equipped with a top-shelf transporter, gear, and crew. Gobert had one of the 1997 factory World Superbike mounts, while teammate Thomas Stevens rode a kitted Vance & Hines machine. Ferracci's team looked comparatively underfunded, with Tom Kipp and Mike Hale on board. American Honda was represented by ironman Miguel DuHamel and partner Ben Bostrom, the new young gun. Suzuki looked strong, with Mat Mladin and Aaron Yates on the trusty GSXRs, and Muzzy Kawasaki again fielded defending champ Doug Chandler and Tommy Hayden. A strong cast of stars and supporting players.

When the curtain opened at Phoenix, Gobert smoked the field, pun intended, and was trailed home by the Mladin and Yates Suzukis. At Daytona for the annual Scott Russell benefit, Chandler was second and Gobert limped to eighth with an overheating engine. The contest soon condensed to combat between DuHamel, Chandler, and Gobert, but a brutal crash in New Hampshire deleted the Honda rider with injuries. Then Gobert was disqualified from the World Superbike round at Laguna Seca for failing a mandatory drug test, and Bostrom logged impressive fourth and third places. A week later Gobert flunked the AMA urinalysis and was handed a one-year suspension, which was later reduced on appeal to three races. Chandler, de-tuned by a nasty crash at Laguna, struggled as young Ben Bostrom continued to compile points. The two were tied going into the final event in Las Vegas, but Chandler's luck squirted away in an oil leak and Bostrom took the championship, without having won a single race.

the aerodynamics at the rear, you have to fix the front, because if the front doesn't work, the back doesn't work. And to make the front work you need to have a bit of a more covering fairing, which is the opposite of what people have been doing up to now. The 916 fairing could be bigger, but this is where you run into the perceptions of

The 1999 996 S came in 18 pounds under the standard edition, a loss attributed to the Marchesini five-spoke magnesium racing wheels, lighter frame, Ohlins racing steering damper, and numerous carbon fiber bits and pieces. The S model had seating for one only, and a $4,500 higher price tag.

Ducati Performance was the name, and World Superbike Championship was the game. Carl Fogarty put the logo at the top again in 1999, zooming to his fourth title. Ducati Performance, the parts and accessories division, incorporated Gio.Ca.Moto in 1998 with Daniele Casolari in charge. Bill McMillan

World Superbike was a more accommodating venue for Ducati in 1998, especially since John Kocinski had departed for a Grand Prix ride on the Movistar/Sito Pons Honda. But the scrap was still between Ducati and Honda, with Fogarty gunning for a third title in a new Ducati Performance team managed by Davide Tardozzi; 1996 champ Troy Corser, back from the GP battles, teamed with Pierfrancesco Chili in the Ducati Corse team under Virginio Ferrari. Quite an arsenal. Castrol Honda had replaced Kocinski with the torrid Texan Colin Edwards, with ever-zealous contender Aaron Slight as teammate. Noriyuki Haga on the Yamaha and Akira Yanagawa on Kawasaki added drama to the proceedings.

With two former titlists on Ducatis, and Chili as covering fire, it appeared that Bologna could fairly well keep the war in-house. Fogarty and Corser were 1-2 in the opener, but then Haga blasted to three wins in a row, followed by Edwards scoring his first and second Superbike wins at Monza. Next Chili and then Slight claimed top of the podium, and got in the habit of it. Corser was compiling seconds and thirds, and by the three-quarter mark at Laguna Seca, held a 27-point edge on Slight, with Chili and Fogarty a few points behind. At Brands Hatch, among his enthusiastic fans, and despite wins by Edwards and Corser, the Englishman's season seemed to take focus.

Carl Fogarty has a thousand-yard stare that makes Clint Eastwood's look myopic. Of the two Scots/Irish facial types, pug and hatchet, Fogarty inherited the latter. And the blue-green meanies in his eye sockets look like diamond-cutting lasers. Most often they are actually looking inward, reviewing, rehearsing, rendering each

turn. But on the outside Fogarty takes on the chiseled visage of a hungry peregrine falcon that has just spotted his lunch a half-mile away. Mr. Tenacity they call him, and given the absence of a broken motorcycle, arm, or leg, the predatory birdman of Blackburn, Lancashire, refused to be bested on a racetrack. Even when he was beat he wouldn't stay that way.

The dramatic showdown came at Assen, the penultimate round, with Fogarty trailing Corser by 20 points. In

The cockpit view from the saddle of the Ducati MH900e has been seen by only a select few. The curved triple clamp attaches to a Hyperpro steering damper; the tach sits atop a digital speedometer. The black square left of the speedo is a monitor wired to a video camera in the tail section. Production models got conventional mirrors.

Ducati Stores, featuring Ducati Gear, were launched in Manhattan and have spread to Europe, South Africa, and Australia. Fears among the faithful that the fashion imagery would attract poseurs, trustfunders, and leathered lubbers have been largely allayed by their absence on the backroads. So far.

the first race Chili passed Fogarty on the last lap to win as Corser settled for third. In the second round the Italian tried a bold late-breaking move on Fogarty in the last corner, tucked the front end and crashed. In the paddock afterwards, Chili erupted loudly in Italian and English and tried to punch Fogarty out, and the pair nearly had a full bareknuckle dust-up going when they were pulled apart. Fight fans gave Chili the edge in punching power, but Fogarty still had his helmet on. The hard feelings would

hang on, but Fogarty went to the final race in Japan only 6 points down on Corser and Slight. The dramatic climax evaporated when Corser crashed in practice, breaking three ribs and forfeiting the title; and Slight couldn't get up to speed. Fogarty thus collected his third championship, showing uncharacteristic emotion, and promised to be back with Ducati in 1999.

World Ducati Weekend

Between racing seasons, Ducati management had decided to have a 50th birthday party. Timed to coincide with the Misano race in June, the festivities combined a celebration of success with tours of the factory and new Ducati Museum, rides to and from the Adriatic coast, parties, celebrity shoulder-rubbing, vintage racing, concerts, and picnics—plus a fair measure of good public relations. Surely just about every Ducati rider from Glasgow to Tokyo was there, and most of them rode.

There was a bit of worry over the logistics and the potential for rowdiness; the World Cup Soccer matches were under way concurrently in Paris. "We nearly had a few nervous breakdowns," Minoli admits. "First we didn't know if people were going to show up. Or if they would behave. The Dutch came in Heineken trucks." The German investors, who seemed to be the only people wearing suits, came in Mercedes sedans to have a look at their money in action. Escorted by TPG managing director Abel Halpern, the bankers showed no apparent signs of disapproval.

Aaron Slight knocked the cherry off the top by winning both events at Misano, but the track was host to music, foods, and numerous rides, vendors, and factory-tech seminars. And a mock race between the Ducati team riders and a Minardi Formula One car, with formation wheelies. And a parking lot loaded with Ducatis of every description, and some beyond, with license plates from all the countries in Europe. And a banquet-table selection of speed equipment from bevel to belt eras. And more Monster accessories than anyone might reasonably imagine, beautiful women named Francesca, and the sun sparkling on the Adriatic Sea. *Magnifico, bellisimo!* and this is Perfectly All Right.

Fabio Taglioni, 78, had not been in good health, but the prospect of a Ducati reunion with old friends and fans seemed to rejuvenate him. Dr. T. began walking more and feeling better. Then there they were, on a Saturday afternoon, gathered from the pages of living history into the Italian summer of 1998. Ingegnere Taglioni, Franco Farne, Paul Smart, Leopoldo Tartarini, Bruno

Spaggiari, Massimo Bordi, Giancarlo Falappa, Doug Polen—the mechanics and crew members from three generations of the racing fraternity. Taglioni was clearly pleased, smiling broadly, and moved by the honor accorded him by all those assembled.

Then someone fired up a rorty V-twin, warmed the engine a few seconds, and gradually brought up the revs. Then another engine barked to life, and another. One rider cinched the front brake and spun up a lusty burnout, striking a desmodromic symphony of resonant thunder, tire smoke, applause, and cheering Ducatisti. Tears streamed down Taglioni's face. The gentleman of Bologna heard this musical tribute, played on instruments of his own design, the chorus of his lifetime run, over and over again. It was a father and child reunion, the power and the glory audible. Even non-Italians were weeping.

"This is a company with a tradition of engineers," says Massimo Bordi. "The first was Taglioni, the second myself, and the third with the young engineers. From this period we got three great ideas: the desmo, which came first from Mercedes, but Taglioni put it on a bike; then the 90-degree V-twin came in the seventies, then the trestle frame came with the TT 600. From these three ideas we made great starts, going forward with continuity, heritage, and innovation. The second step was desmoquattro and the first racing bike with an electronic fuel injection system. Third was the water-cooled system, which was new for Ducati, and a new trestle frame with progressive suspension. Step by step we have done this, and now the next step with a new generation. The next step will remain a twin, 90-degree, four-valve, trestle frame.

"We have a great occasion with TPG. In '97–'98 we invested more in the company than in the previous 10

The ST4 was added to the Sport Touring roster in 1999. Offered in red or black, the 916-powered tourist was 22 horsepower up on the ST2 and carried only an additional 13 pounds. The additional tariff for the extra valves, compression, and thrust was only $2,000. The ST2 was $12,500.

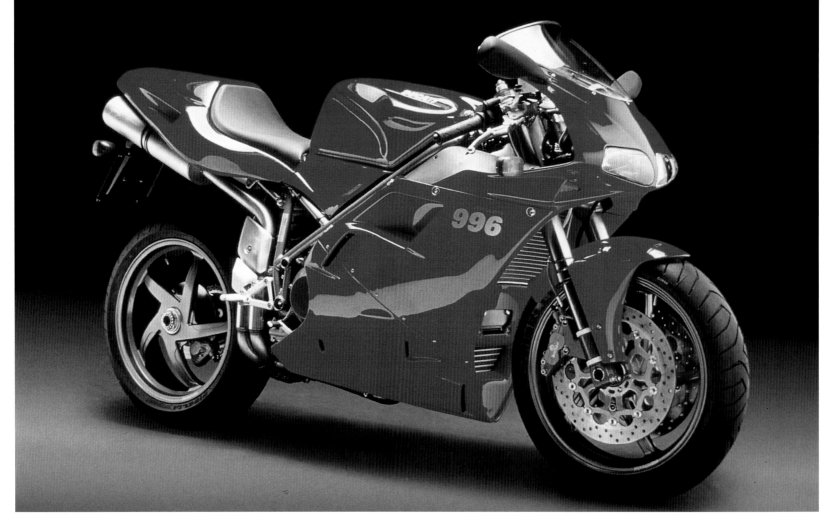

The desmoquattro reached its 15th year of production with the 2000 model 996. The gunmetal gray frame and wheels match the factory racing bikes, and the top-of-the-line SPS matches the racer's steering geometry. Only the standard model (shown) was offered in mono or biposto trim.

The City was one of four new models in the 1999 Monster lineup. Built to serve both the Sunday ride and weekday commute, the City came standard with detachable soft luggage. It shared with the Cromo the high end of the Monster menu, both at $11,000. Both were dropped for 2000.

years. In the past we could not invest enough on new engines, on research and development, innovation; now we are in the position to invest a lot. So from the management point of view, for new engines and products, we have a great occasion. For technical solutions, in any case, this is an Italian company, with a great heritage, with the philosophy to improve, to move ahead, and to respect the heritage. To be innovative, not conservative. Innovation and heritage together; this is the dialectic. And TPG agrees with this philosphy. They do not ask me to make a four-cylinder, or a five-valve engine; they trust me and they are confident that we made the right steps in the past 50 years, and that we will go on doing the best.

"I have spent 20 years of my life with this company, and I love this company more than anything else. But this is the best period ever for this company. At the beginning of the 1990s we had the great success with Roche and the Superbikes, the best competition results ever, the world championship. Now with TPG we have the opportunity to make another big step. In 1998 we invested more than $9 million in racing, more than ever, and we have two teams in World Superbike, two teams in AMA, two or three teams in Supersport. They understand the assets of this company, which are the brand identity, the racing heritage, and the technical differentiation from all the other competitors."

Global Imagery

David Gross, Ducati's director of global image, came to media work through corporate law and financing in New York. As a TPG consultant he worked on the issues of licensing, apparel, Ducati stores, ad campaigns, special projects, and product launches. He admits that Harley's revival didn't go unnoticed in the industry.

"Harley has done an excellent job, and we're putting our spin on it. We feel we have an even richer world to invite people to join; we have racetrack events, club races, Superbike. Where Harley does fashion apparel, we do performance apparel. Where they have HOG meets, we have race meetings. We are really at two ends of the spectrum, but we're the two brands that have the power to attract people.

"Our job is to get closer to our fans and customers. We now have Ducati Performance with Daniele Casolari of Gio.Ca.Moto as director and majority shareholder. We hope to make World Ducati Weekend the European sportbike event of the summer, and we may eventually go to different racetracks around the world, and have the fans ride on the track."

Gross worked to set up the company's flagship stores in London, Sydney, South Africa, and New York. He and fellow young American Kristin Schelter originated the Ducati/People advertising campaign, using factory employees and racers in black-and-white ads. The message was: We are the people who make Ducatis, and we ride them. We are not fashion models even though this is a fashionable ad. This campaign was a real improvement on the previous one, and it got attention.

Peter Egan, *Cycle World* editor at large, has been a Ducati enthusiast for some 25 years. "Some traditional Ducati fans are a little worried that the whole Ducati cafe and boutique stuff are being overdone," he says. "I don't know if that's going to be a problem or not, for those who like a little lower-key approach. On the other hand I think their public relations effort in the past was probably a bit underdone. Especially considering the history they had to draw on, and the good looks of the bikes and so on, it was something that could use more exposure. I don't think it hurts them to have a nice ad with Fogarty sitting on his bike. They're doing a better job of getting out posters and brochures that help people get drawn into a dealership. Everybody's watching to see what will happen, but so far it seems pretty positive. But we'd rather not be told it's a lifestyle decision.

"I think they've blown the styling on the new Supersport a little bit, but that's just my opinion. I know probably seven people who own the old 900 SS, and nobody is planning to buy a new one. There are always 900 SSs for sale. I think that's because people are attracted to them because they look nice, and then they ride them for a while and realize it's not a Honda. I think that happens to a fair number of people. It's like getting a severe sports car of some kind and then discovering what they really needed was a Honda Civic.

"I just got a 996. Did a track day at Elkhart Lake and got in about two and a half hours of track time. It's a very uncomfortable bike for daily use, not much fun in town, but when you get out in the country and up to speed, the wind takes the weight off your wrists. When you're riding it fast or you're on the track, it's just perfect. It's like a perfect tool.

"I actually dragged my knee for the first time at Elkhart Lake on the 996. I had to build up speed, too, and the bike is fast. Elkhart is a fast track, so you're really carrying some speed into corners. I was getting up to about 142 on the front straight going up the hill, and that's a lot of speed to lose when you come into turn one there. To judge and make sure you don't put yourself off the road.

"I ran into Kevin Cameron at Daytona in the pits and asked him what was looking good. He said if you look at everything else and then look at the Ducati, they have

The 900S was also among the new 1999 Monsters, fitted with a steering damper, adjustable suspension, and sporting Michelin TX tires. Offered only in black on black, the bad boy Monster survived the cut for 2000 and became the new top-dollar dude. The Monster Dark was still $7,000.

Anthony Gobert (left) and Ben Bostrom made Vance & Hines Ducati the team to deal with in AMA Superbike in 1999. Despite different styles in hair, riding, and just about everything else, the young guns shared a persistent itch to be at the front. But Suzuki's Mat Mladin won the championship. Bill McMillan

riders who know what they're doing. So when they have a specific problem, like not enough off the bottom, they come up with an answer. Then they have too much off the bottom, then they fix that; and they proceed in a series of incremental fixes. Which I think has made Ducati suit the World Superbike circuit the way the XR Harley fits dirt.

"The motorcycle has all kinds of things you could regard as problems; it has a fair size valve angle, they're commited to that desmodromic business which has to give them some problems, and they've got their weird weight distribution, with that horizontal cylinder that shoves the mass of the engine way to the back. On real low-speed racetracks, they'll push. But they handled that a different way; rather than have a crash program to make a 60- or 72-degree Vee, they said let's smooth out the power. If the power is really smooth, then it won't upset the front tire. And they come off the corners strongly anyway.

"The Twins versus Fours thing goes back a long way. Big Stevie Wonder (McLaughlin) was one of the people who talked to the FIM when they were setting that breakup." When World Superbike began, Ducati was a company with more history than product. And the FIM, like Ducati, is a European organization; and knowing what we know about organizations, we shouldn't be surprised that they decided to give them not only a displacement break but a weight break. But Ducati has shown what a crew of clever, knowledgeable, and experienced people can do with a basic piece of hardware. As opposed to the kind of Lockheed approach that Honda has used, which is to say we'll put a thousand engineers on it and hose the problem down with money. You can get results that way, but they aren't necessarily as thoroughly considered as Russian results, where they don't have unlimited amounts of exotic materials. They don't have a lot of computer technology, but they've got time to think about the problem.

"The Japanese saw that twins were hot in the market. They didn't look at why, they only looked at 9.8x66 mm bore and stroke, 90 degrees, red in color, multitubular chassis. Those hot buttons were pressed and the results were not a firestorm in the marketplace. Even at a low price. Of course what Ducati and Harley-Davidson do is sell the buyer not so much a piece of hardware, as a legend into which he or she can step. Whereas the Japanese are in a kind of commodity business, and everyone has to see these problems in their own paradigm. Ducati has a motorcycle that is exhibited in museums, and talked about by half-knowledgeable people

evolved into a perfectly rational, everything-in-its-place racing bike. It looks like everybody else is just working with hoses and wires and lines. And I think of that when I pull the bodywork off the 996; there's a lot in here, but they've put it all in such a small, refined package. I go out to the garage and turn the light on and look at that 996, and it just knocks me over every time I see it again."

Kevin Cameron, technical editor at Cycle World, is the author of Sportbike Performance Handbook, and a veteran tuner and moto-scholar. "I think Ducati is rather like Rolls-Royce in the aviation business. They're the supreme developers. For many years I had all this respect for designers; this person with far-seeing understanding has drawn an engine that has all this capability to be developed into something far beyond the original conception. Wasn't that wonderful? But in fact, it frequently happens that a great design, like the Rolls Merlin V-12 aircraft engine, was drawn by a competent person and then developed with incredible attention to detail (and government money, in their case) into something absolutely amazing. The power rose by a factor of 2.4, from 1938 to the very end.

"I believe that Ducati has simply done what they had to do next, and in elaborating on a 15-year-old design, which to the Japanese might seem an excercise in futility, they've gotten to know it the way the NASCAR boys know their small-blocks.

"They don't have to have a complete new durability program every 15 minutes, and they've got some good

from fashionable addresses in New York as art, and that can't hurt them.

"But these people with boutique phobia are always going to feel less special. The guys whose tattoos don't come off in the shower are furious because Harley is now a yuppie bike. Well, nothing is forever. Enjoy the things that are good while they're good, and step out of it. People are enjoying Ducatis right now, and if these Texas people screw it up somehow or turn it into a commodity, or miss the boat and it all goes down the drain, it still will have been fun."

Turning the Century

Ducati brought along more fun for 1999, with an eight-valve iteration of the ST2 appropriately labeled the ST4, the civilian version of the 996, and a trio of Monsters in new outfits.

The ST4 featured the 916 engine with a healthy horsepower bonus over the two-valve model, and an additional $2,000 tacked on the price. More spirited sport-tourists also got an improved air intake system, high-output alternator, and remote brake and clutch reservoirs. The shift levers and sidestands were new and improved, and metallic blue was an optional color choice. Saddlebags, however, were not included in the tariff and went for an additional $800. Without the bags or a passenger, top speed was a respectable 150 miles per hour.

But the new 996 was the headline news. The 916 had changed little in five years, and the grapevine buzz on a new 75-degree twin with variable valve timing, or even pneumatic poppets, remained unconfirmed. Italian grapes are traditionally slow to mature. So the 996 came forth as the final example, maybe, of the original desmoquattro first offered in 1988. The big-bore motor had been available in the 916SPS, but the production model was on the floor at $16,500 and boasted a number of improvements. Higher compression, stronger crank, new clutch, and an enlarged intake and exhaust system were standard issue. The engine gained 5 horsepower on top and 10 in the middle, a handful more midrange wheelie urge, and pulled right up to 162 miles per hour. The 916's brakes were wonderful, the 996's larger ones fantastic.

The 996 got twin injectors per cylinder, but they were still managed by the 916's direct processor rather than the sequential system in the SPS. And the limited edition's Ohlins shock was displaced by a fully adjustable Showa unit. The 996 was offered in single- or double-seat versions, although passenger accommodations

were minimal. The 996S, single seat only, came fitted with a lighter frame, Ohlins shock and steering damper, Marchesini five-spoke wheels, carbon fiber fenders, and airbox for another fistful of lira—in red only. "The ultimate street-legal Superbike." And only $21,000.

The Monster roster multiplied in 1999. The 750 and 900 Dark joined the 600, Europe's best-selling motorcycle, with a matte black tank and fenders on a gloss black frame and wheels. The price leader at $7,700, the basic

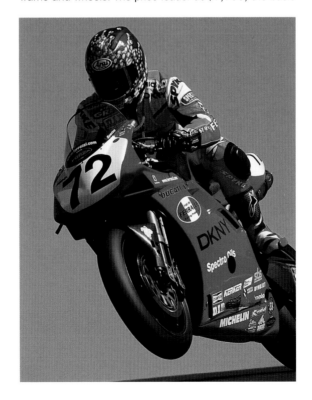

Bostrom's extraordinary learning curve grew even steeper with Gobert as the exemplar of aggression. Here he trails the Aussie at Willow Springs, conducting his own research and development. In 2000, Ben receives advanced training on the unfamiliar tracks of Europe, under Headmaster Fogarty.

Larry Pegram sneaked up on the factory boys at Willow Springs, and put the Fast By Ferracci Ducati atop the podium. Tire choice won the day, but the Ohio dirt-tracker showed continuing poise and perseverance. Personal coaching was provided by former Grand Prix Champion Kevin Schwantz. Bill McMillan

chrome-plated fuel tank. All members of the Monster family shared the new jumbo alternator, and the 900s got larger valves. With six models in the lineup, the M series had established the worthiness of versatile V-twins at affordable prices. Monstrously successful.

Bologna also continued expanding the coverage of Ducati Stores in Europe, Australia, South Africa, and the United States. An intranet communications system was designed to connect stores with each other and the factory, and a Ducati Stores website was implemented near the end of the year. Ducati Gear was launched in the fall of 1998, charged with development and marketing of Technical and Safety Apparel lines, and in-house creation of a casual Enthusiast selection of clothing. With Dainese, well-known maker of racing leathers as partner, Ducati Gear offered Fogarty replica and Safety Pro one-piece leathers, two-piece suits, and Gore-Tex jackets and pants. Wardrobe selections included gloves, boots, and a new Ergon racing helmet.

The new Ducati Performance catalog listed an array of go-fast goodies and accessories. Here one could find the titanium connecting rods, humpy cams, Marchesini magnesium wheels, clutch kits, performance exhaust systems, piston kits, and carbon fiber furbelows beyond measure. The Ducati lovers' Christmas list. There is no sanity clause.

Few disagree that Anthony Gobert is an exceptionally skilled racer, and perhaps the most naturally talented rider to appear in some time. Less common ground is apparent on the issues of his attitude, lifestyle, and sense of responsibility. At the end of 1999 he was without a ride for 2000 but later signed with Bimota. Bill McMillan

black 750 found quick success as a platform for custom paint jobs, accessories, and hot rod parts. The 900S appeared as the sporty of the *familigia Mostro*, with adjustable shock, steering damper, sport fairing, carbon fiber fenders and panels, and sticky Michelin tires. The Monster City, sensibly attired, addressed the sport-commuter segment with higher bars, clear windscreen, comfy passenger seat, and detachable soft bags by Mandarina Duck designers. And the Cromo reflected admirers in its

Without Kocinski to provide incentive, Foggy shows due diligence and a measure of caution at Laguna Seca. But despite his lack of fondness for the circuit, he could hardly be considered one of the slower riders in attendance. Bill McMillan

The next order of business for the TPG was to go public. Ducati Motor became a publicly owned company in March 1999, when TPG posted 60 percent of the stock on the New York Stock Exchange. The ADR, representing 10 common shares, opened at $32 and raised $255 million. The stock fluctuated only slightly for the rest of the year.

Some analysts think that Ducati stock is undervalued, although most may not be familiar with the ebb and flow of fortunes in the motorcycle market. Those who invested in Harley-Davidson stock in the late 1970s or early 1980s, and were scorned at the time, now have reason for contentment. Those who may have had a substantial stake in the recent $100 million attempt to revive the Excelsior-Henderson marque are less comfortable. Predicting the next economic groundswell in the motorcycle business is akin to doing the same thing in rock 'n' roll, movies, or toys. Which is to say, guesswork.

Racing into the Millennium

Ducati's AMA Superbike program looked superb as the 1999 season opened. The Vance & Hines team was, as ever, a well-equipped and adept group of veterans. Anthony Gobert was back, on probation, and still usually the fastest man on the track. Teammate Ben Bostrom, having won the 1998 title without a race victory, was hungry for his first win, and he had the benefit of Gobert as the lead bunny rabbit. It all looked quite promising.

Contrary ideas were exhibited by Mat Mladin, most audible of the Aussies, and his swift Suzuki. Other interested parties included the evergreen Doug Chandler on the always-potent Muzzy Kawasaki, Jamie Hacking on a Yamaha R7, and Mike Smith and young Eric Bostrom on RC45 Hondas. Fast By Ferracci, demoted to reserve status by the factory-financed Vance & Hines effort, had Larry Pegram and Matt Wait on factory bikes. And Pegram had former world GP champ Kevin Schwantz as a coach. This, agreed street-bike racing enthusiasts, should be interesting. And it was.

Gobert got to business early and won at Phoenix over Mladin. But with at least six riders capable of victory on a given day, the racing was close and rough. Mladin proved most consistent and came to the sixth race double-header at Road Atlanta with a healthy lead. But Gobert and Bostrom ran 1-2 in both rounds and gained ground, while Mladin scored 3-6. The series leader was nearly wiped out by an ambulance that appeared on the track in the wrong place at the wrong time. Gobert missed a practice round at Loudon, and

considered not racing there for safety reasons, then showed up a day late and set a new track record. But Doug Chandler won the race.

One of the season highlights came at Laguna Seca, where the AMA riders faced off with the World Superbike

After losing the 1998 championship in a last-race crash, Troy Corser was set to take his second world title in 1999. The former AMA and World Superbike champ did well at Laguna Seca but hard luck dogged him again and he finished the season third, just behind Colin Edwards.
Bill McMillan

Like most racers, Fogarty shuts everything else out when it's time to set up the bike, qualify, or go racing. Off the track, though, he holds no special fondness for the litany of questions and cameras; he's a civil bloke without pretensions.
Bill McMillan

stars. Carl Fogarty had won both opening rounds in South Africa, marking his 50th Superbike victory. At Monza, in fierce racing with Colin Edwards and Frankie Chili, the Englishman added two more, and in Germany he split wins with Troy Corser. Coming to Laguna, Fogarty held a substantial point lead over Corser, but was hardly keen on dicing with the local talent; Corser had done well at Laguna Seca before, and Fogarty had never liked the track. As a points-saving exercise for the Europeans, Monterey became an intermural battle between Gobert and Bostrom and the first round went to the Australian marvel. He was leading the second when he

crashed, letting Bostrom and Chili through to decide the outcome. At the end young Ben put a bold move on the aggressive Italian, up the inside at the entrance to the Corkscrew, and won his first Superbike race. Corser edged Chili for second, but with Fogarty fourth the Aussie gained a meager six points toward the title.

Like Fogarty, Ben Bostrom came to racing with a genetic directive. His father owned a Honda shop and raced, and Uncle Paul was an accomplished dirt-tracker. Ben started riding at age four, racing at eight, but didn't begin roadracing until 1995. In 1998 he became the first rider to win the AMA Superbike title in his rookie season. Bostrom had planned a long racing career with Honda, but the Ducati offer had certain appeals, including that particularly Italian patina of glamor, bravado, and really good food—along with plenty of cash.

The scrap between Suzuki's Mat Mladin and the Vance & Hines Ducatis carried through the season, and only five points separated them going to Mid-Ohio. By the final round in Colorado it was between Bostrom and Mladin, whom Paul Carruthers of *Cycle News* called "the hardest working man in AMA roadracing." Although he had only one win during the year, consistency put the Aussie in the lead at the end. Bostrom needed a win, with Mladin well downfield to put Ducati on top, which didn't happen. Mladin's tenacity won him the championship. Gobert called in sick for the final race, and showed up healthy a few days later at a race in Australia. The unpredictable Antonio "Go-Show" Gobert was expected to join Carl Fogarty on Ducati's World Superbike factory team for 2000. If the deal ever was seriously under consideration, it evaporated in Colorado. Three weeks later, Ben Bostrom signed to ride with Fogarty in Davide Tardozzi's team. Steve Rapp and Australian Troy Bayliss were hired to ride the Vance & Hines Ducatis in AMA Superbike.

World Superbike again provided Ducati a prominent international platform in 1999, and Fogarty opened the season with double wins at Kyalami in South Africa. The defending champion's competition came from teammate Troy Corser, and once again the Castrol Hondas of Aaron Slight and Colin Edwards. The Texan started slowly, having crashed in testing at Laguna less than two weeks before the opening race.

At Donnington, Fogarty and Edwards each had a first and third, which moved Edwards closer to Corser who was second in points. Noriyuki Haga took the R7 Yamaha to its first win at Albacete, Spain, and was narrowly edged by Edwards in the second race. Fogarty logged a third and fourth, gaining a 36-point margin on Corser, who rode injured to sixth and seventh places. Two wins at Monza put him even further ahead, and Edwards' two second-place finishes moved him past Corser to second in points. In the second race, the Brit's margin on the Texan at the finish line was .005 of a second.

Fogarty and Corser split wins at the Nurburgring, where Edwards crashed in oil in the first race. Several riders fell in the same turn, and poor officiating was blamed for the accidents. Edwards' misfortune allowed Corser to move back into second in the points race. Rain turned the Austrian A-1 Ring into something of a circus, with 16 riders sliding off. Edwards and Chili each topped the podium once, but Fogarty's second and fourth places stretched his lead even further, and Corser's first race crash allowed Edwards to close to within one point of him. An estimated 30,000 of Fogarty's British fans crossed the channel for the race at Assen, Holland, and their hero responded with two hammering victories. Troy Corser, who had set a new lap record, and Aaron Slight finished 2-3 in both rounds.

So it came to Hockenheim, and the penultimate event. Lap averages at the German speedbowl are close to 125 miles per hour and drafting is a necessity. Carl Fogarty needed only a good finish to secure the title, and his second to Aaron Slight in the first round gave him his

fourth championship. King Carl performed cartwheels for the fans (not on his motorcycle). The second race became the dice of the season. Slight, Edwards, Fogarty, Chili, and Yanagawa edged away from Meklau and Corser, and the fivesome ran in shifting formations the

Chili swapped wins with Foggy at Albacete, Spain, in 1998. He went on to trade off with Slight in Germany, win both legs in South Africa, and win one round at Assen. But five DNFs hurt and he ended fourth in points. Chili was a veteran at 33, but still quick as anyone on a given day. Bill McMillan

Ben Bostrom's career story had taken on the characteristics of a fairy tale: Polite, handsome lad wins the AMA Superbike championship on a Honda in his rookie year; signs with the high-powered Vance & Hines Ducati team for 1999, gets Ducati factory ride in Europe for 2000. Hollywood stuff. Tod Rafferty

entire race. Their ballistic ballet went down to the wire; Yanagawa, Slight, and Chili running hard in front, Fogarty slipping through into third, then second. Then first. But Chili ran it in underneath on the final lap to take the lead, and the Alstare Suzuki's first dry-track victory. Dramatic stuff. Fogarty's exclamation point on the season, Chili's joy, and the Castrol Honda riders' continuing despair.

New Centurions

The 2000 model year produced no new Ducatis and few modifications to the existing lineup, feeding speculation that a few striking additions will appear for 2001. The 900 and 750 Supersports got new front disc brake carriers, master cylinders, and braided steel lines. The handlebars went up 12 mm, the windscreen was elevated to enhance comfort, and the hinky sidestand was replaced by a nonself-retracting unit. Both models were fitted with lighter three-spoke alloy wheels.

The Superbike menu offered three models each for both the 996 and 748, with standard, sport, and racing editions. The 748R (formerly SPS) got the trick heads and valve timing to make peak horsepower at 500 fewer rpm, aided by race-style "shower form" 54-mm throttle bodies. The 996SPS, also monoposto only, gained no power increase, but the Marchesini five-spoke wheels, aluminum subframe, and a lighter battery excised about 6 pounds. The 43-mm Ohlins fork, with lower axle mount, gave the SPS the same steering geometry as the racing bikes. The gunmetal-gray frame and wheels also matched the color schemes of the competition machines.

The Monster, which now accounted for 43 percent of Ducati sales worldwide, displayed minor styling changes to the tank and tail section and slightly higher handlebars. All models got the 43-mm inverted Showa fork, stronger front brakes, and a new sidestand. The 900S was awarded 900 SS cams, fuel injection, and the close-ratio 748 transmission. The sporty Monster also received the gunmetal-gray frame and wheels of its racier brethren. The desmoquattro *Mostro* is expected to arrive in 2001.

The two- and four-valve 2000 Sport Touring models got new graphics, a two-layer clear coat, and a Kryptonite anti-theft lock under the seat. They also received a power connector for heated garments, cell phones, and such. The ST4 was granted the gunmetal hues, a larger 180/55 rear tire, and a 996 instrument panel with electronic tach.

Will the Supermono, in road, track, and supermoto trim, be on display at the Milan Show in September 2000? And what of Ducati's own version of the Cagiva Gran Canyon dual sport, or the Monster SS, or the carbon-fiber framed 999 75-degree pneumatical do-dah deluxe? We shall see. . . . Perhaps. Do not worry. *Domani.*

We Will Always Race

By its own speedometer, Ducati entered the new millennium at warp speed. The international investment appeal of "branded luxury goods" has provided the booster rockets, but the main engines run on the rich Italian mixture of tradition and sporting enthusiasm. Fifty years is a good run for any motorcycle company,

Jim Leonard (left) confers with Anthony Gobert on the setup for Laguna Seca. The native of Wollongon, Australia, set the fast time on a partially moist track. He would win the first round in California and slide out in the second while chasing Bostrom and Chili. Tod Rafferty

let alone an Italian outfit, and the younger employees seem to hold a healthy respect for the heritage in place at *Borgo Panigale*. Their performance will determine if the Bolognese ballet can carry on well into the twenty-first century.

On the other hand, Ducati no longer has the market cornered on Italian style. Its very success has sparked a renascent motorcycle industry throughout the country, and Bologna now comes into direct competition with Cagiva, restructured and restored to financial health. Aprilia has shown gathering strength with its two-stroke roadracers and Superbike V-twin Mille. Laverda is demonstrating some muscle with its line of sportbikes, and even Italjet has entered the arena with a sub-400 pound roadster powered by the 900-cc Triumph triple. Even the French are building stylish sporting machines. The French! So the new millennium bodes well for the gourmands of continental moto cuisine. *Buono appetito.*

Surely the Japanese will respond with a banquet table of their own, and their protean engineering and production capacities will ensure that the menu continues to carry a wide selection of choices, with pricing that remains within some reasonable framework. Ducati and Honda came of age concurrently in the past half-century, to quite different effects of course, but they retain the commercial symbiosis of being both adversaries and colleagues. The fact that Honda brings the new RC51 V-twin to the Superbike grid this year testifies to the tacit agreement that sporting competition is good for one and all, and that "street bike racing" has come of age.

Ducati has, for a company so often at the edge of extinction, been well served by racing. The competition efforts were largely responsible for their salvation by Cagiva, which allowed the continued development of the V-twin. Then, as Cagiva foundered and TPG brought Ducati back up to speed, the racing enterprise would remain in the forefront and soon be upgraded. Race-what-you-build, and vice-versa, has somehow survived in Bologna for nearly a half-century, and no corporate policy change seems imminent. The lineage from Taglioni's 100-cc Gran Sport of 1955 runs almost unbroken up to the 996 Superbike of today, but has rarely produced any state of financial security, let alone abundance. In Italy the distinctions between life, art, and commerce have remained vaguely drawn, or even unnecessary. Ducati has done remarkably well in sustaining the tradition.

"We've always raced," says Massimo Bordi. "Components can be tested without racing, but we still need racing triumphs to promote our company image. And then there is still our passion for racing. We will always race."

INDEX